San Antonio

365

≋ On This Day in History ≋

David Martin Davies
AND
Yvette D. Benavides

Maverick Books
Trinity University Press
San Antonio

Published by Maverick Books, an imprint of
Trinity University Press
San Antonio, Texas 78212

Cover design by Sarah Cooper
Book design by BookMatters, Berkeley
Author photo by Jenna-Beth Lyde, Texas Public Radio

Printed in Canada

ISBN 978-1-59534-916-3 paperback
ISBN 978-1-59534-917-0 ebook

Image credits by page: iStock/HairFacePhoto: 11; General Photograph Collection,
UTSA Special Collections: 21, 86, 121, 144, 203; University Health System archives:
27; Texas State Capitol: 34; Center for American History, University of North
Texas: 40; Library of Congress: 50, 60, 106, 109, 128, 136, 161, 230, 261, 278, 283;
Nan Palmero: 57; United States Air Force: 67; iStock/Nikki Blumberg: 96; iStock/
KenWiedemann: 153; 25or6to4, licensed under CC BY-SA 3.0, color edited from
original: 168; Analy Diego and Ronald Rocha: 175; Pixabay/skeeze: 184; iStock/
sasacvetkovic33: 191; Paramount Pictures: 201; Howard Kelly: 212; Texas Public
Radio: 223; Reynold Brown: 234; iStock/BeteMarques: 246; Zetpeo202, licensed
under CC BY-SA 4.0, color edited from original: 251; NASA: 271.

Trinity University Press strives to produce its books using methods and materials
in an environmentally sensitive manner. We favor working with manufacturers
that practice sustainable management of all natural resources, produce paper using
recycled stock, and manage forests with the best possible practices for people,
biodiversity, and sustainability. The press is a member of the Green Press Initiative,
a nonprofit program dedicated to supporting publishers in their efforts to reduce
their impacts on endangered forests, climate change, and forest-dependent
communities.

The paper used in this publication meets the minimum requirements of the
American National Standard for Information Sciences—Permanence of Paper for
Printed Library Materials, ANSI 39.48–1992.

CIP data on file at the Library of Congress

24   23   22   21   20 | 5   4   3   2   1

For Elizabeth Rozier Davies—
my mother who loved San Antonio and fought to preserve its
history, protect the aquifer, and feed the homeless

and

for Christianna L. Davies—
our daughter who will continue to write San Antonio's stories

Stay off the gobbledygook language.
It only fouls people up. For the Lord's sake,
be short and say what you're talking about.

MAURY MAVERICK

Introduction

It was June 17, 1937, and San Antonio mayor C. K. Quin was attending the funeral of Charles Bellinger, the man known as the "Black Boss of San Antonio."

Newspaper photographers waited for the mayor to step out of what was then known as the "Negro Municipal Auditorium." Holding his hat in front of his face, the dapper Quin ordered his bodyguards to shield him from the cameras. "If he clicks a shutter, take him down," one police officer was told.

Bellinger and Quin were unlikely partners who controlled San Antonio. Quin, an associate of the Ku Klux Klan, ran a disciplined political machine that kept him and his allies in power. It was reported that he used the city health department to run prostitution rings, illicit liquor sales, gambling operations, and rigged elections. Bellinger, a professional gambler, racketeer, bootlegger, and businessman, was given sway by the city's white power structure because he could deliver the black vote. His death was a political problem for Quin. The two had a symbiotic relationship. Both were mired in questionable practices, but both became part of San Antonio's long history of progress during a critical time.

History is full of ordinary days made extraordinary when we observe them through the rearview mirror. Hindsight affords us a perspective that those who lived these experiences could never have imagined. Future generations will shake their heads at today's moments, at San Antonio's inefficient bureaucracies and its statistics surrounding the peril that befalls women in what we consider modern, enlightened times. They will also marvel at the spirit of compassion that emerges from every major disaster a city can survive.

How do we judge the actions of a wide swath of players over three hundred years? Hindsight can render a borrowed wisdom that comes from eschewing the corrupt machinations of figures like Quin and Bellinger even as we learn how they somehow managed to help the city along. Bellinger, for example, made sure that African American schools were funded and that East Side neighborhoods received city services. This attention to black neighborhoods did not occur during this time in Houston and other cities. Quin also finessed a transaction that brought a $34 million no-cash deal for the city to acquire the electric utility that would become CPS Energy.

San Antonio 365 tells the city's history in day-to-day episodes that, taken as a whole, weave together a nonlinear narrative capturing a character of San Antonio that is rarely expressed. A vignette for each day of the calendar is snipped from the larger record of events, and monthly reflections by Yvette Benavides ruminate on the struggle and strife of the many characters in a wide-ranging story. Common themes emerge, as resonant and real today as they have been for the past three hundred years.

A vast majority of these stories were sourced from San Antonio's newspapers, the *Express* and the *Light*. The problem with newspapers of the past is that the poor and communities of color were rarely given ink—unless they were presented as problems of society and perpetrators of crime—and these newspapers are no exception. As products of the pre–civil rights era, they not only reflected but also reinforced the oppression of the times.

Journalism is the first draft of history. It provides the first rendering of events as lived, witnessed, and reported. Our hope is that *San Antonio 365* captures the excitement of city-shaping events while also showing how they shaped the city we live in today. Many of these stories are well-known, while others have been plucked from the mists of almost forgotten history.

Some characters make multiple appearances. In the early to mid-twentieth century Quin and Bellinger, but also Maury Maverick and Emma Tenayuca, were colorful individuals who heavily influenced the city when it was home to gangsters, corrupt police, crooked politicians, gamblers, and bootleggers. There are recurring themes, too—stories about the San Antonio Public Library, the city's charter, the public utilities, public health, and the local infrastructure.

San Antonio was shaped by daily struggles to achieve a municipal system that serves the greater good. As the struggle continues toward an age of fairness and equity, we would be wise to remember that bigotry and narrow-mindedness are part of the city's past. History teaches us that we are doing better, day by day.

JANUARY

Saint Anthony, for whom San Antonio, Texas, is named, is the patron saint of lost things. The evocation of his sympathies can be a spiritual or secular petition for what's missing. Most people know what it's like to stand in a room where every bookshelf has been rummaged in a fruitless search for that one volume, or the couch cushions have been upturned to reveal a retired remote and loose change but not the car keys you swear you'll designate a spot for next time—if only Saint Anthony will help you find them. You slip your hand into the pocket you know you already checked, twice, and there they are, the muscle-memory-familiar feel of the faux leather fob, one key to the car, the other to the front door.

The informal version of the prayer goes something like this: "Tony, Tony, turn around. Something's lost and must be found." Others of us talk directly to the patron saint of lost things, appealing to his sympathies and making deals in our spinning minds, our mouths cotton-dry in the anxiety of these interminable empty-handed moments.

Saint Anthony might best be known for being the patron saint of lost things, but he is also known for his powers of preaching, abilities so miraculous that even fish, submerged below the surface, understood him from their murky pond, kept in thrall during a sermon at first rejected by heretics. The only surviving relic of

Saint Anthony is his tongue, which remains in the basilica named for him in Italy. When it was found, it was reported to be incorrupt, as wet and pink as it had been in life.

The reason we invoke Saint Anthony's help when something is lost can be traced to an incident that occurred in Bologna. A book of Psalms that contained his notes and comments went missing. His life and times in the 1600s, of course, predate the printing press, and any book was an irreplaceable item of great value. Anthony prayed fervently that the book would be found, and the thief who had taken it was moved to return it.

Saint Anthony seems an ideal patron saint for those of us who have reached a certain age, who walk back into rooms and look around searchingly for what we can't remember walking in there for in the first place.

San Antonio has reached a certain age now, too. At the ripe old tricentennial, she's aged well, a classic beauty, spry as ever, keeping up with the kids on the latest trends and innovations. It's as if she's aging in reverse, an ever-burgeoning Benjamin Button metropolis.

There are, of course, some episodes over the past three hundred years that San Antonio might like to forget. However, enough of those chapters remain in recorded history, documented for posterity, to tell the story of what emerges as mythological in moments, magical in others.

History isn't what happened—not on its own. History is what we remember, what we retell and write down. To study the past, historians will tell us, is to unlock the prison of the present.

History is not just the stories of heroes in quiet, unopened textbooks; it's lived by ordinary people and happening on every street all the time.

On January 11, 1954, San Antonio attorney Gustavo "Gus" Garcia successfully argued before the U.S. Supreme Court. The storied "class apart" case, *Hernandez v. Texas*, focused on the exclusion of Mexican Americans from juries in some seventy Texas counties. In 1948 Garcia had argued *Delgado v. Bastrop ISD* in U.S. District Court, the outcome of which made the segregation of Mexican Americans in Texas public education illegal.

Garcia, the first valedictorian at Thomas Jefferson High School in 1932, went on to study at the University of Texas at Austin. Like Saint Anthony, he had the gift of extemporaneous elocution, but he was hardly as austere as the Franciscan friar. His auspicious beginnings and illustrious career were eclipsed by the merciless grip of alcoholism, and he died of liver failure at age forty-eight. He was destitute at the time, his tremendous talents dissolved by demons that had put him in and out of mental institutions. He was lost—perhaps any

petitions sent on his behalf to Saint Anthony went un-
heard—and yet his story is immortalized, part caution-
ary tale, part hero's journey.

It happens that way sometimes in matters of faith
and destiny.

History humanizes the spectral figures of the pow-
erless, like those served by Gus Garcia's mental might
and the fullness of his potential before he succumbed
to a poison as strong as the fear and loathing that sim-
mers in a segregated space. In a real sense, Garcia was
a patron saint for Mexican Americans lost in the chaos
of inequality. We've always known that the lives of the
saints were most cruel, their sacrifices all the more pre-
cious for it.

January 1, 1941

Owen Kilday is sworn in as Bexar County sheriff. Kilday,
who would become the county's longest-serving sheriff, was San Antonio's chief of police until Mayor Maury
Maverick fired him in 1939. After Maverick raised his
hand to take the oath of office, he pointed at Kilday and
said, "You're fired." Kilday was elected sheriff a year later,
and the two continued their public political feud. Kilday
ran a political machine for hire that used deputies to collect votes, monitor polling sites, and harass opponents.
Called the "High Sheriff of Bexar County," he was known

for his brutal tactics against San Antonio's minority population and anyone he suspected of being a Communist. His police officers used billy clubs, tear gas, and water hoses against the pecan-sheller strikers of 1938. Kilday designed the badges that are still used today by the San Antonio Police Department and Bexar County Sheriff's Office. He died on August 12, 1962, while serving as sheriff and was eulogized as the "greatest lawman in San Antonio history."

January 2, 1952

San Antonio sees the first full day of a new style of city government, run by a city manager under the direction of a nine-member city council. On October 2, 1951, voters approved by a two-to-one margin the adoption of the city charter that scrapped the previous model with a strong mayor and four dedicated commissioners. The old charter was recognized as allowing lack of governmental oversight and accountability, which led to blatant institutional corruption and inefficiency. Promising to make San Antonio "the best run city in the nation," C. A. Harrell was hired as the first city manager. Eyebrows were raised, however, over his $30,000 annual salary, which seemed lavish for the day. Harrell lasted a year and a half before being ousted in a donnybrook over sick pay. For his last month on the job, he was paid one dollar.

January 3, 1913

The San Antonio, Fredericksburg and Northern Railway Company is chartered with the mission to connect Fredericksburg with the San Antonio and Aransas Pass Railway Company. The railroad was the product of twenty-five years of dogged determination by the citizens of Fredericksburg to establish a railroad connection. Because of the Hill Country's rolling terrain, construction required building twenty-four bridges, one per mile, and digging a tunnel 920 feet long, one of only six railroad tunnels built in Texas. The service ended in 1942. The tunnel remains and is now home to millions of bats at Old Tunnel State Park, ten miles southeast of Fredericksburg.

January 4, 1858

At a distance of thirty feet, Capt. W. G. Tobin shoots an apple off the head of a visitor from New York City. William Gerard Tobin, a Texas Ranger, soldier, and businessman, was born in South Carolina and traveled to San Antonio in October 1853 with his brother Dan. Tobin served as city marshal of San Antonio and, in 1859, as captain of a company of San Antonio militia volunteers; he was then commissioned a captain in the Confederate army. After returning to San Antonio after the war, Tobin leased the city's former U.S. Army headquarters, which had been used by the Confederacy. He converted the building into the Vance House, a hotel that stood on the site of today's Gunter Hotel. He also became an enthusiastic promoter of Texas-style Mexican food and founded a canned chili con carne factory with the U.S. Army and Navy as customers.

January 5, 1945

San Antonio is declared free of smut, obscene books, and nude calendars. The Catholic Legion of Decency pronounced that the city had been scrubbed of offensive material and deviant literature after a month-long inspection of local newsstands, according to a report by city commissioner P. L. Anderson. After receiving a complaint from the legion, Anderson ordered San Antonio police to seize any obscene material being peddled in the area. The legion said their next goal was to clean up the Spanish-language films shown on the city's West Side. They said obscenities had been eliminated from English-language films in town, but they had not been able to sanitize the Spanish films.

January 6, 1931

San Antonio's Bicentennial Committee abandons the proposal to erect a statue honoring the arrival of the Canary Islanders. Instead the committee chose to place a large granite boulder in Main Plaza with a bronze plaque that would be dedicated at the official celebration on March 8. Committee members told the public there wasn't sufficient time to have a statue made. A group of fifty-six Canary Islander settlers had arrived at the presidio of San Antonio de Béxar on March 9, 1731, and founded the villa of San Fernando de Béxar, joining a Spanish military and civilian community that had existed since 1718.

January 7, 1937

San Antonio chief of police Owen Kilday orders all bookie betting joints in the city closed following a complaint made by Raymond Russell, the operator of Alamo Downs, a horse racetrack west of the city. Russell said bookies were damaging his pari-mutuel betting business. Alamo Downs, with seating for five thousand, opened to great acclaim in 1934 and ran races on a mile-long track. It effectively closed in May 1937, and that same year the Texas Legislature outlawed pari-mutuel betting. Alamo Downs became a horse training track and an auto-racing venue but was abandoned by the 1950s.

January 8, 1839

Samuel Augustus Maverick, a Texas lawyer, politician, land baron, and a signer of the Texas Declaration of Independence, is elected mayor of San Antonio. Maverick's name is the source of the term "maverick," which means "independently minded." In 1842 Maverick was captured along with others by invading Mexican troops in San Antonio and marched to Mexico. He was offered his freedom if he would denounce Texas independence—which he refused to do. Eventually he was freed and returned to Texas, bringing with him the chain that held him in prison and the gourd he drank water from.

January 9, 1842

San Antonio is in a panic over fear of Mexico's reconquest of Texas. Mexico refused to recognize the Republic of Texas's independence after the revolution and the Treaties of Velasco. The fledgling nation was in constant fear that Mexican forces were coming to reclaim the lost territory. That fear became reality on January 9, 1842, when General Mariano Arista issued a letter from Monterrey announcing his plan for invasion. He promised amnesty and protection to Texans who remained neutral in the upcoming struggle. It would be two more months before the Mexican troops arrived in San Antonio.

January 10, 1887

Maj. Jacob Lyons is given command of the Excelsior Guards, a volunteer battalion of African American infantry in San Antonio. Lyons was born into slavery on the Mapp Plantation in Virginia in 1844. During the Civil War he enlisted and served in the U.S. Army in Key West, Florida. Throughout his tenure as a commanding officer, he organized training camps and precision drill exhibitions and led parade marches through downtown San Antonio and other Texas cities. The guard frequently won first prize in drill competitions across the state. Lyons pressed the state for support for African American citizen-soldier troops and was able to negotiate equipment, rations, and pay for the troops from the U.S. Army during their four-day encampments at San Pedro Springs.

January 11, 1954

San Antonio attorney Gustavo "Gus" Garcia argues before the U.S. Supreme Court. The case of *Hernandez v. Texas*, also known as the "class apart" case, focused on the systematic exclusion of Mexican Americans from juries in at least seventy Texas counties. In 1948 Garcia filed the suit *Delgado v. Bastrop ISD*, which made illegal the segregation of Mexican American children in Texas public education. In *Hernandez v. Texas* the Supreme Court unanimously decided that Mexican Americans had equal protection under the Fourteenth Amendment. Garcia's argument was so compelling that Chief Justice Earl Warren gave him sixteen extra minutes for his argument.

January 12, 1943

The Hertzberg Circus Collection and Museum debuts at the San Antonio Public Library. Local attorney and state senator Harry Hertzberg created one of the nation's largest collections of circus memorabilia, including items from P. T. Barnum, Tom Thumb, and Buffalo Bill's Wild West. The extensive collection, including a large catalog of rare books, initially filled two large rooms in the city's public library at Market and Presa Streets, now the Briscoe Western Art Museum. When the library moved to 203 South Saint Mary's Street in 1968, the circus museum took over the entire building. The museum closed in 2001, and the collection was released to the Witte Museum.

January 13, 1943

The city of San Antonio dismisses its censors. Two watchdogs of indecency were removed from the city's payroll when city commissioner P. L. Anderson noted they were unnecessary. "We have a national board of censors and a League of Decency," he told the *San Antonio Light*. In addition to the two paid censors, there was an unpaid, ten-member censoring board that was created by ordinance on May 14, 1940. Local censors said they would keep an eye out for objectionable material in major motion pictures and would censor scenes that insulted the sensibilities of San Antonians. They also monitored carnivals, burlesque shows, and "cheap movie theaters."

January 14, 1965

The Sir Douglas Quintet records "She's about a Mover," with a catchy Vox Continental organ riff delivered by Augie Meyers and soulful vocals by lead singer and guitarist Doug Sahm. The song, clocking in at two minutes and five seconds, follows a twelve-bar blues structure with a Tex-Mex sound. This was during rock's British Invasion, so the San Antonio band adopted an English-sounding name and style in hopes that it would help sell records. The song was a smash hit. The original lyrics were "She's a body mover," but that was perceived as too risqué for radio airplay.

January 15, 1977

After electing city councilmembers on a citywide basis for twenty-five years, voters approve district representation. With 20 percent voter turnout, the change to the city charter barely passed. It was called the ten-one plan because it included ten single council districts and one citywide office for mayor. Opponents said it was unworkable because councilmembers would squabble over their districts' needs at the cost of working for the city's overall benefit. Overwhelming support from Mexican American voters on the city's west and south sides delivered the victory. The single-district plan was advocated by the U.S. Department of Justice, which noted that San Antonio city leaders had violated the Voting Rights Act by annexing north side areas to dilute Mexican American voting strength. In the initial district elections, five Latinos and one African American won seats on the council, a city hall majority.

January 16, 1980

The biggest cowboy boots in the world are assembled in San Antonio. Standing forty feet high and stretching thirty feet long, the "ostrich skin" boots were designed by Austin artist Bob "Daddy-O" Wade. But they were originally built for a 1979 project in Washington, D.C. Three blocks east of the White House there was an open space, and the nonprofit Washington Project for the Arts wanted Wade to step in. The artwork was later purchased by North Star Mall and rebooted there.

January 17, 1976

San Antonians vote four to one in favor of stopping construction of a "super mall" over the Edwards Aquifer recharge zone. The special referendum was spurred by the Aquifer Protection Association's petition drive to override a city council zoning vote. The landslide election made protecting the city's source of drinking water an issue city leaders would have to deal with. A follow-up campaign calling for the public purchase of Bexar County's recharge zone failed, however.

January 18, 1974

LoVaca, a pipeline subsidiary of Coastal States Gas Producing Company, announces that it is doubling the cost of natural gas for San Antonio's electric utility. LoVaca had signed fixed-price contracts to supply San Antonio and other South Texas cities with natural gas. With energy prices soaring and supplies dwindling, the subsidiary could not meet its contractual obligations, at one point cutting off gas supplies to San Antonio and Austin during the winter. With the leadership of Mayor Lila Cockrell, San Antonio sued LoVaca and Coastal States and in the settlement created a company that would locate its headquarters in San Antonio. That company is Valero Energy Corporation.

January 19, 1987

San Antonio holds its first official Martin Luther King Jr. March. On January 15, 1970, the city council first recognized King's birthday with a resolution and a moment of silence. The council instructed the city manager to study the possibility of renaming a street after the slain civil rights leader, but a motion that the city observe January 15 as a holiday in King's memory failed without discussion. Texas first celebrated Martin Luther King Jr.'s birthday as an official state holiday in 1991. It had become a national holiday in 1985.

January 20, 1881

The *San Antonio Light* newspaper begins publication. The afternoon daily and Sunday morning paper was a longtime rival of the *San Antonio Express*. In 1924 William Randolph Hearst bought the *Light* and brought in the Hearst policies and editorial point of view. The local newspaper rivalry continued until October 6, 1992, when the Hearst Corporation purchased the nonunion *San Antonio Express-News*. Hearst announced it would close the *Light* if it couldn't find a buyer, and the final issue was published on January 28, 1993.

January 21, 1931

Vaudeville stars and conjoined twins Daisy and Violet Hilton win their independence. Once the highest-paid

GERMAN-AMERICAN DAY.

A Gorgeous Dream of the Past.

A Splendid Pageant Illustrating the Initial Point
of the Great Germanic Race.

In Its March Westward, It Spread Into Various
Streams, Reaching from the North Seas.

At Last Coming Face to Face With the Malay, in the
Person of the North American Indian on Columbia's
Shores.

Looking Backward Over Centuries, the Cradle Lullabys
of the Race Come Up Sweet and Fresh as
Songs of Birds From Forgotten Woodlands.

"Father Rhine" Reclining in Majesty, Pours His
Stream of Life Over the World.

Each of the sixteen magnificent
floats is a poem of the race, but the
pageant must be looked at and
studied from a broader view than
simply a German allegory, pertaining solely to that German people
. . . At the same study. For
there was a time, back of the old
legends . . . when the term
Germans meant . . . s and applied to all the peoples marching
westward from the common cradle
of the Caucasian race.

FLOAT NO. 1

"Germania and Columbia."

Is a fitting introductory to the
Parade ; it is the consummation of
the history of the race, in its strides
toward the setting sun.

Germania, the illustrious, from whose
bosom has sprung.
The mightiest of heroes, of which poets
have sung.
Presents in the bright Union of Columbia's stars
Her youngest best bravest, in peace and
in wars.

FLOAT NO. 2

"Beowulf Kills the Sea Monster"

[Beowulf Legend, 3rd Chant.]

This legend is one of the oldest
of German traditions, and is beautifully illustrated by the gorgeous
float. The rather literal translation from the German tells the
story of the legend:

"A spotted monster, with greedy grasp,
Dragging me down to the watery main.
Tried to devour me, but by fortune's
charm
And a good sword blow, was slain.

Wolfdeitch in the Moorland Swamp.

[Beowulf Legend, 7th Chant.]
The man now recognized the heaving
Soreground,
Full of boiling blood.
And saw in the water the serpentine
dragons,
Coiling and twisting off in the mire.

In the foam of the billows
The hero killed one with his weapon,
Down to its heart the hard steel he

performers on the vaudeville stage, the Hilton twins were born on February 5, 1908, in Brighton, England, to an unmarried barmaid who immediately rejected the girls. The sisters were joined by their hips and buttocks; they shared blood circulation but no major organs. The mother's employer, Mary Hilton, saw the infants as a money-making opportunity and essentially bought them. As part of the Hilton household, the twins were exhibited in the back rooms of bars and then as carnival sideshows while being physically abused and trained to be stage performers. After Mary Hilton died, she bequeathed the twins, as if they were personal property, to her daughter Edith Meyers, and Edith's husband, Meyer Meyers, a former Australian balloon salesman, who moved the group to San Antonio, where they lived in a mansion when not on the vaudeville circuit. In 1931 the sisters sued the Meyerses for their independence in Bexar County, and the case was covered by newspapers around the world. The twins testified that they were kept in "bondage" and detailed the abuse they had suffered under the Meyerses. They sought an injunction and the proceeds from their shows. The court ruled in their favor, and they gained freedom from their contract and $100,000 in damages.

January 22, 1991

The Texas Supreme Court rules for the second time on *Edgewood v. Kirby* and again asserts that the property tax system of public school funding is unconstitutional. The case was first filed in 1984 by parents from San Antonio's Edgewood Independent School District, who charged that the state's method of funding public schools discriminated against students in poor school districts. A year later, on January 22, 1992, the Supreme Court of Texas voted seven to two that the legislature's funding fix was illegal. In 1993 the "Robin Hood recapture" plan was adopted, requiring property-wealthy school districts to share funding with property-poor school districts. The debate over school funding continues.

January 23, 1913

San Antonio's Fourth Ward Health Auxiliary petitions the city council to come up with a sanitary way to dispose of household garbage. They complained that the neighborhood open garbage pit was no longer adequate. The organization also approved its "Ten Commandments of Public Health and General Welfare of the People," which included admonitions to citizens to cover garbage cans, cut weeds, and plant trees, as well as the directives "Thou shall clean out the habitation of thy horse" and "Verily, verily, thou shalt pay thy poll tax tribute" for necessary municipal improvements.

January 24, 1905

The Texas House of Representatives passes H.B. 1, titled "An Act to provide for the purchase and conveyance to the State of Texas of the land in the City of San Antonio known as the Hugo, Schmeltzer & Company property." This was the so-called long barracks of the Alamo, which dated back to the Alamo's days as a Spanish mission and was being used as a dry goods store. The state reimbursed Clara Driscoll $65,000 for purchasing the structure a year earlier to save it. In 1883 the state had paid the Catholic Church $20,000 for the old Alamo church. Landscaping and a post office on the north were added to the plaza in the late 1800s.

January 25, 1955

The Maverick family goes to court to stop San Antonio from building a parking garage at Travis Park. The city planned to create four downtown underground parking lots, at Main Plaza, La Villita, Alamo Plaza, and Travis Park. In 1870 Samuel Maverick had bequeathed his orchard as a city park. In 1955 his descendants claimed that if the city used the land for anything but a park they would regain ownership. The city insisted that it could use the land for any purpose. But Maverick, true to his name, never had a formal deed to the land; the gift to the city was an oral agreement. The Mavericks lost the case, but the publicity generated by the court battle created public pressure that forced the city to give up on the garage.

January 26, 1924

The Ku Klux Klan operates a three-day rodeo and carnival at the San Antonio speedway south of the city. The Klan had hoped to stage a parade through downtown with members from across the state. Fearing bloodshed and clashes with the local population, however, the city council refused to issue the organization a parade permit. San Antonio was one of the few Texas cities not controlled by the Klan. Regardless, the Klan held its rodeo, which included initiation rituals and a cross burning.

January 27, 1944

Army private Sow Kunihiro recovers his seized personal property. The *San Antonio Light* described Kunihiro as a "Jap Alien" in a story explaining that Kunihiro had been targeted by the U.S. government after war broke out with Japan and that his personal items had been confiscated. Kunihiro had lived in south San Antonio before joining the army. He presented his dog tags as identification to the U.S. Marshals office and recovered his pistol, ammunition, radio, and camera.

January 28, 1947

Bob Luby and his cousin Charles R. Johnston open the first Luby's Cafeteria at 517 North Presa Street. At the time San Antonio was home to thousands of servicemen and their families, many of whom lived downtown. The cafeteria had twenty-five employees and seated about 180 people. A second cafeteria opened in Alamo Heights in 1948. By 1959 the company, incorporated as Cafeterias, Inc., was operating nine cafeterias in Texas. By 1982 the company was listed on the New York Stock Exchange and operated sixty-three cafeterias, mostly in Texas. By 1990 the firm employed 9,500 workers at 175 locations in ten states. On July 16, 2004, Luby's announced that it would move its headquarters from San Antonio to Houston.

January 29, 1917

The Robert B. Green Memorial Hospital opens to the public. Named for Bexar County's progressive county judge and state senator, this charity and teaching hospital opened its doors at a critical time. San Antonio, then the largest city in the state, was bursting with new arrivals fleeing the Mexican Revolution, and was also hosting the amassing of U.S. Army troops preparing for America's entry into World War I. Soon after opening, the hospital would face the great influenza epidemic of 1918. Establishment of the Robert B. Green was the first powerful step in the creation of the University Health System, which has become an internationally recognized academic, research, and health care provider.

Robert B. Green Memorial Hospital, 1917

January 30, 1967

The space race turns deadly in San Antonio with two air-men killed at Brooks Air Force Base. Richard Harmon and William Bartley Jr. were tending to research animals in a simulated space capsule when a spark ignited the pure oxygen atmosphere. The circumstances surrounding the Brooks fire were tragically similar to those of the Apollo 1 accident, which happened three days before and took the lives of astronauts Gus Grissom, Roger Chaffee, and Ed White. White was a San Antonio native and the first American to walk in space. The cause of both flash fires was the use of a 100 percent oxygen atmosphere in the space capsules. Researchers at Brooks had previously warned about the dangers of a pure oxygen environment, observing that in addition to being extremely volatile, pure oxygen caused wire insulation to flake apart, which would provide the spark to trigger a fire. Their warnings were overruled by NASA.

January 31, 1938

After learning of a 20 percent pay cut, twelve thousand pecan shellers, known as *nueceros*—most of them women—walk away from their jobs and initiate a bitter three-month strike. At the time San Antonio accounted for half of the nation's pecan production. Shellers' pay was two or three dollars a week, making their work one of the lowest-waged jobs in the country. Working conditions were difficult. Without plumbing and ventilation, the job was associated with a high tuberculosis rate. Local labor and civil rights leader Emma Tenayuca was elected to lead the strike. The city responded by mobilizing 250 law officers to patrol the West Side, and police chief Owen Kilday made more than seven hundred arrests to break the strike. Eventually producers agreed to pay the minimum wage established by the Fair Labor Standards Act.

FEBRUARY

February is the time of year when most San Antonians have grown weary of our abridged South Texas winter. We're ready to mothball the corduroy pants, and we long for the days of shorts and *chanclas*. (How brief our memory of the canicular days of 100 degree temperatures and steamy afternoons.) We look forward to Fiesta and all that is portended by the shortest month of the year.

In Shakespeare's *Much Ado about Nothing*, Don Pedro asks Benedick what ails him: "Why, what's the matter, / That you have such a February face, / So full of frost, of storm and cloudiness?"

On February 12, 1961, a group of African American college students stood in the box office queue at the Majestic Theatre to see the film *The World of Suzie Wong*. They looked into the February faces of those rejecting their admission through the main doors and pointing the way to a separate entrance and relegation to the balcony. They confronted a cold shoulder, a frosty reception, and a frigid recalcitrance from those who refused to acknowledge their peaceful protest.

A warmer day in June 1955 did not melt the resolve of the ticket takers, who watched as the Rev. S. H. James, head of the local NAACP chapter, led picketers in front of the Texas Theatre (which once stood at 105 E. Houston Street) to protest its segregation policy. African

American patrons were told they could enter the theater but must sit only in the mezzanine and balcony. *Carmen Jones* was showing, an adaptation of the French opera featuring an all-black cast, but this didn't assuage what these peaceful protesters faced in the theater foyer or elsewhere in the city.

To discuss this contentious moment in history without considering the films in question would mean missing the finer point of the prevailing representations of people of color in popular film. In *The World of Suzie Wong*, for example, William Holden plays a white savior leading man to biracial actress Nancy Kwan, the call girl with a heart of gold whose exotic features attract multiple characters and whose immorality can only be legitimized by their overtures to her. She asks to be Holden's "permanent" girlfriend, implying that they will remain together even outside the context of his own displacement in Hong Kong—even, say, in the United States.

James Baldwin reviewed *Carmen Jones* in his essay "Life Straight in de Eye," giving an unflinching and acerbic critique of the Otto Preminger production. The cast, which featured such luminaries as Dorothy Dandridge, Pearl Bailey, and Harry Belafonte, did little to deflect Baldwin's slings and arrows. "A movie is, literally, a series of images, and what one sees in a movie can really be taken, beyond its stammering or misleading dialogue, as the key to what the movie is actually involved in saying," he wrote. He added that the film does little to help audiences relate more pointedly to the black characters and their story lines, although it does lead them to question "the interior life of Americans." Baldwin asks if blacks would simply remain ciphers in Hollywood and, therefore, in the American collective consciousness. He allows that to be a cipher might be more appealing than alternative representations for blacks in film.

Let's presume the irony in each of these peaceful protests. What protesters were fighting for was a place at the table, a seat of their choice in the theater. The other concerns would be handled through the 1960s and beyond.

In May 2019 the touring company of the Tony award–winning musical *Hamilton* attracted thousands to the front doors of the Majestic Theatre. Lin-Manuel Miranda, a man of Puerto Rican descent, composed the music. The company featured people of color in the roles of this country's founding fathers, including an Asian George Washington and black and Latino statesmen.

On those warm May days, the kind that herald weeks of summer and sunshine, people from every walk of life brandished e-tickets on cell phones, took the elevator to the merchandise tables, sipped wine from plastic cups, and settled in for the show. On that day everyone was allowed in the room where it happened.

February 1, 1946

Lackland Air Force Base is designated the Army Air Force Military Training Center. This made San Antonio the home of basic training for the Army Air Forces. The center was created on July 4, 1942, when the War Department separated part of Kelly Field into an independent installation. The first class of cadets began training there in November 1941, weeks before the attack on Pearl Harbor. After World War II the base was considered for decommission but was instead given a new mission. On July 11, 1947, it was named Lackland for Brig. Gen. Frank D. Lackland.

February 2, 1836

Col. William Travis arrives in San Antonio with a small cavalry and takes command of the fortifications of the Alamo. Several weeks earlier it had been frontiersman Jim Bowie's decision to ignore Gen. Sam Houston's order to abandon the Alamo. Bowie didn't want the cannons to fall into the hands of Mexican forces, and he reasoned their defense could delay Santa Anna. Also on this day, Bowie wrote in a letter that he would "rather die in these ditches than give San Antonio up to the enemy."

February 3, 1924

William Jennings Bryan blasts whiskey, atheism, and evolution in a speech at San Antonio's Beethoven Hall. The

Portrait of James Bowie, c. 1825

former secretary of state was introduced to the crowd by Texas governor Pat Neff, who called him an "unyielding defender of truth." Bryan used the platform to tell the crowd that atheists shouldn't be allowed to teach or hold public office. The man known as "the Commoner" also ridiculed Charles Darwin and evolution. "There is nothing funnier to me than the guesses made by scientific guessers," he said. Bryan closed his remarks, however, by praising science for being able to make war "more intensely murderous."

February 4, 1892

An inspection of the Southwestern Lunatic Asylum, now known as San Antonio State Hospital, focuses on the problems the facility is having with its water supply. The artesian well was producing 180,000 gallons of undrinkable water a day. It came out of the ground sulfur-saturated and at a temperature of 103 degrees. Although the water was undrinkable, Charles Scheuermeyer found another use for it. He established a resort nearby, the Southwestern Park and Hot Sulphur Natatorium. Two years later McClellan Shacklett used the natural resource to found the Hot Wells Hotel and Spa. The spa's popular mineral-rich water treatment attracted the era's rich, powerful, and famous to San Antonio.

February 5, 1877 \\

Construction is completed on train tracks connecting San Antonio to the industrial world. At the time San Antonio was one of the largest cities in the nation without a rail connection, and community leaders knew if this wasn't corrected soon the city would irreparably suffer; the population was already dropping. In January 1876 Bexar voters approved $300,000 in bonds to pay the Galveston, Harrisburg and San Antonio Railway to bring in the Sunset Route. The city's first regular train service on the line was on February 16, 1877. A cheering crowd of eight thousand, half the city's population, turned out to welcome the iron horse with a massive celebration and torchlight parade.

February 6, 1901 \\

This day is believed, as far as anyone can tell, to be the last time the outlaw duo Robert LeRoy Parker and Harry Alonzo Longabaugh was seen in San Antonio. The pair, better known as Butch Cassidy and the Sundance Kid, occasionally frequented Madame Fannie Porter's brothel at the corner of San Saba and Durango Streets in the city's Second Ward. The brothel had a reputation for providing the luxuries of silk sheets and chilled champagne and served as a hideout for outlaws on the run. The story has it that this is where Cassidy made his famous bicycle ride. Porter threw the "Wild Bunch" one last party the night before they left to rob a bank in Wagner, Montana. The Pinkerton Agency began rounding up the outlaws soon after, and Cassidy and Sundance left for South America.

February 7, 1974

George Gervin plays his first game as a San Antonio Spur. Gervin joined the American Basketball Association's Black and Silver under a cloud of cloak-and-dagger intrigue. The deal with the Virginia Squires involved brown paper bags of cash, secret negotiations, and an attempted double-cross. When the twenty-one-year-old "Iceman" came to San Antonio, it was a gamble. His first night at the Convention Center Arena, Gervin scored twelve points, but the Utah Stars won. Then the Spurs won thirteen of the next eighteen games and headed to the playoffs. Gervin's play transformed the team, so much so that they joined the NBA and Gervin was headed to the hall of fame.

February 8, 1830

José Antonio Díaz de León, the last Franciscan missionary in pre-republic Texas, reluctantly complies with a decree from the Mexican government that the old Spanish missions be secularized, which meant that missions across Texas were to be turned over to diocesan authorities. The increasingly numerous Anglo settlers wanted to control the mission properties, but Díaz de León argued that the mission Indians still needed protection. After years of resistance he finally surrendered to the order and, as he expected, the mission lands were soon made available to colonists.

February 9, 1931

Texas folklorist and writer J. Frank Dobie lectures at San Antonio's Main Avenue Senior School. The topic: the history of the Texas longhorn. Dobie, considered one of the state's most significant literary figures, called the longhorn the most important animal in Texas history. In 1941 he would publish the book *The Longhorns*, which was a critical success. Dobie's writing was instrumental in saving the longhorn from extinction.

February 10, 1939

A basketball game riot and citywide racial tensions erupt after a championship match between rival segregated high schools. Longtime dominating Brackenridge Eagles, a whites-only school, squared off against the Lanier Voks, a high school for Mexican Americans on the city's West Side. Lanier's Tony Cantu sank the winning basket in overtime and Eagles fans stormed the court, assaulting Voks players in a free-for-all fight. Police reported there were more than a hundred people in the melee. One student received a knife wound in the chest, and eight police squad cars were called to the game to escort the Voks team bus to safety. Lanier coach Nemo Herrera led the Voks to state championships in 1943 and 1945.

February 11, 1908 \\

Adina de Zavala defends the Alamo's long barracks from destruction, barricading herself in the dirty, rat-infested warehouse for three days. She was determined to save the Alamo compound from what she called "business greed." A deputy sheriff was sent to drag her out, but she refused to leave. "I'll stay here forever if need be," she told him, and in turn, he did not allow her to have any food over the course of the three-day siege. Once her attorneys had worked out an agreement to temporarily turn over the structure to the governor, she emerged.

De Zavala's grandfather Lorenzo was the first vice president of the Republic of Texas. Adina had moved to San Antonio with her family in the 1880s and taught elementary school as a young woman. A self-described "student and jealous lover of Texas history," De Zavala applied her energies toward saving the Alamo and the other Spanish missions. She also worked with the San Antonio Conservation Society and other groups to ensure the rescue of the Spanish Governor's Palace in Military Plaza.

Adina de Zavala, 1910

February 12, 1961

An attempt is made to desegregate the Majestic Theatre. African American college students stood in line to buy tickets to the film *The World of Suzie Wong* and rebelled against the practice requiring black patrons to use a separate entrance and sit in the balcony. They were turned away, and they went to the end of the line to try again. The action was peaceful, with no arrests. Over the next three months there were more stand-ins and blocked attempts to integrate, until the Majestic finally abandoned Jim Crow. Other San Antonio theaters soon followed.

February 13, 1913

Ignacio E. Lozano Sr. founds *La Prensa*, a Spanish-language daily newspaper, to address the needs of the growing number of Mexicans in exile in San Antonio. Mexico was engulfed in a bloody revolution, and *La Prensa* became political refugees' link between their homeland and their new city. In 1926 Lozano would establish another Spanish daily, this time in Los Angeles—*La Opinión*. The papers were platforms that exposed abuses against the Mexican community, discussed civil rights, and promoted democratic ideals.

February 14, 1916

Second Lt. Dwight D. Eisenhower of the Nineteenth Infantry Regiment at Fort Sam Houston proposes to

Mamie Doud. The two met while Mamie was visiting with her parents from Denver. For an engagement ring, Ike gave Mamie a miniature of his West Point class ring, amethyst set in gold. He was twenty-five, and she was nineteen. They married less than five months later and settled into the lieutenant's living quarters at Fort Sam Houston. In 1953 they moved into the White House.

February 15, 1915

The city council proposes a crackdown on troublesome jitneys. "Jitney" was slang for a nickel, the fare for the proliferating Ford Model Ts that were roaming the streets. Some jitneys were freelance bus services that were little more than freight trucks. They were fast and cheap but also a threat to public safety and competition to the streetcars. In March 1915 the city passed an ordinance requiring drivers to have a license, insurance, and a security bond.

February 16, 1861

The Civil War almost begins in San Antonio with a confrontation at the Alamo. The Committee for Public Safety, the local pro-secession militia, surrounded the U.S. Army Garrison at the Alamo and ordered Gen. David E. Twiggs to surrender his troops and the armory. Twiggs could have refused and ordered his men to defend the Alamo. That would have meant a bloody military confrontation, however, and would have been the opening shots of the Civil War. Instead he complied, and two months later the war erupted at Fort Sumter. Twiggs's motivations could have been influenced by his loyalty to his native Georgia.

February 17, 1950

A western parade kicks off San Antonio's first San Antonio Rodeo and Livestock Exposition. Horses, buckboards, stagecoaches, and buggies clattered through the downtown streets along with marching bands and beauty queens. This was the first year the new Bexar County Coliseum, later renamed the Joe and Harry Freeman Coliseum, housed the event. The facility was dedicated "to the pioneers of the Southwest, to the breeders of good livestock, to 4-H and FFA members, their parents and teachers. And all the people in this state who love good livestock." Today the exposition is one of the city's largest annual events, with more than two million visitors each year. It is also one of the top Professional Rodeo Cowboys Association rodeos in the nation.

February 18, 1969

Homemade leaflet bombs explode at about 5 p.m. in Alamo Plaza and the Northwest Shopping Center, shooting flyers some fifty feet into the air and scattering them to the tops of nearby trees. The Minutemen, a conservative political group, claimed responsibility. No one was injured. The flyers declared "Death to socialism" and "Stop the bureaucratic tyrants" and warned that gun registration would lead to gun confiscation: "When liberal Washington bureaucrats and their helpers come for them let'm have'm between their eyes." The Minutemen also warned of an imminent armed invasion of the country by Communists. San Antonio congressman Henry B. González laughed them off. The ultrasecret group had previously threatened the Democrat with the warning "Traitors beware, we have your necks in the cross-hairs of our rifles."

February 19, 1917 〰〰〰〰〰〰〰〰〰〰〰〰〰〰〰〰〰

Gen. Frederick Funston dies suddenly. The fifty-one-year-old was the commanding general of the U.S. Army's Southern Department and oversaw the massive military force along the southern border during the "Border War." A controversial national figure, Fighting Fred Funston was best known for his roles in the Spanish-American War and the Philippine-American War, where his actions were awarded the Medal of Honor. Shortly before U.S. entry into World War I, President Woodrow Wilson had planned for Funston to head the American military action in Europe. Fate had other plans, however. Funston's last moments were spent listening to an orchestra play the Blue Danube waltz in the lobby of the Saint Anthony Hotel. "How beautiful it all is," he said, and then suffered a heart attack and collapsed. Maj. Gen. John "Black Jack" Pershing, Funston's subordinate, was then named the commander of the American Expeditionary Forces on the Western Front in World War I.

February 20, 1973 //

Four weeks after the U.S. Supreme Court rules in *Roe v. Wade* to nullify the Texas law that banned abortion, it is announced that an abortion clinic will open in San Antonio. Planned Parenthood San Antonio founded the state's first legal abortion clinic available to indigent women. Reproductive Services, located at 1106 McCullough Avenue, opened on March 1, 1973. "Heretofore only wealthy women could get safe abortions, while women in lower income brackets were forced to accept bargain basement abortions, which are dangerously performed," Alan Guttmacher, national president of Planned Parenthood, said. He was also quoted as saying that "illegal abortion is a cancer that is the most common cause of female death in the world." The clinic would only accept women who were no more than eleven weeks pregnant and charged a maximum of $165 for the outpatient procedure.

February 21, 1885 //

Desperate outlaws Charles Yeager and James Pitts attempt an escape from a train. The pair were given life sentences for robbing post offices, and Marshal Hal Gosling was escorting them by train to San Antonio. Pitts's family was also on the train, including his grandmother, who slipped him two pistols during a tearful hug. Near New Braunfels, gunfire erupted. Gosling and a deputy were killed. The conductor opened fire and killed the grandmother. Chained together, the outlaws jumped from the train. Pitts died from gunshot wounds, and Yeager was arrested by a posse and sent to prison.

February 22, 1861

The Knights of the Golden Circle holds its state convention in San Antonio. The KGC was a mid-nineteenth-century white supremacist secret society with the goal of creating a nation made up of the southern United States, Mexico, Central America, and the Caribbean—a vast golden circle of slave-holding territories. On this day, the San Antonio KGC "castle," a chapter made up of many of the city's prominent citizens, was active in verbally attacking the pro-Union *Alamo Express* newspaper and leading an overt voter intimidation campaign for the next day's statewide referendum on secession.

February 23, 1861

Texas holds a referendum on secession, marked by ballot stuffing, miscounting, brow-beating intimidation, and other election irregularities in favor of the pro-slavery faction. Witnesses in Bexar County reported that supporters of the pro-secession Knights of the Golden Circle patrolled polling stations and "marked any man who dared to vote against secession." San Antonio voted by a slender margin, 562 to 535, to remain in the Union, but Bexar County voted 827 to 762 for secession, with three precincts not reporting any votes. More importantly, of course, the state had supported secession by a huge margin, 46,153 to 14,747. Nearby Blanco, Gillespie, Medina, and Uvalde Counties voted against secession. The central area counties were pockets of pro-Union support, with German farmers firmly opposed to slavery and the coming Civil War.

February 24, 1914

All of San Antonio's saloons are closed for twenty-four hours during a special election to reform the city's charter. Mayor Clinton Brown supported amendments he claimed were necessary for progress and the city's welfare. He told voters the new charter would provide improved streets, sewers, and a commission form of government, and that the new brand of home rule would create a more stable city government "without the disturbing and harmful effects of frequent city elections." The slate of amendments passed overwhelmingly by a margin of four to one. The commission was inaugurated at city hall in June 1915 and became known for institutional corruption, patronage, and infighting.

February 25, 1971 〰〰〰〰〰〰〰〰〰〰〰〰〰〰〰〰〰〰〰

Local state senator Joe Bernal speaks out at the Harlandale Civic Center in support of a "permanent voter registration law" for Texas. In 1966 the U.S. Supreme Court found that the poll tax in state elections violated the Equal Protection Clause of the Fourteenth Amendment. In response, the Texas Legislature enacted a law requiring voters to register annually. This was seen as burdensome and a deliberate mechanism to limit voting in Texas, particularly for low-income citizens and communities of color. In 1971 the legislature eliminated the annual registration requirement and adopted a continuing registration system.

February 26, 1906 〰〰〰〰〰〰〰〰〰〰〰〰〰〰〰〰〰〰〰

The city council proposes a method for naming San Antonio streets. The old Spanish names would be kept for the existing streets in the First, Second, and Third Wards. The naming system would be applied to new roads by city ward. The Fourth Ward would use the names of trees and plants. Streets around the Alamo and leading into the Fifth Ward would take the last names of Sam Houston, William Travis, Ben Milam, and other Texas independence heroes. Letters and numbers would also be used for Fifth Ward street names. Streets near U.S. government facilities and in the Sixth Ward would receive names of presidents and other "men of national fame." The names of cities and states would be used for the Seventh and Eighth Wards. The city council unanimously adopted the ordinance on March 12, 1906.

February 27, 1868 〰〰〰〰〰〰〰〰〰〰〰〰〰〰〰〰〰〰〰〰〰

The clock tower at the Ursuline Convent is erected. The three-faced clock was brought from France and built above the dormitory building. The Ursuline Sisters (the Daughters of Saint Angela) founded their Catholic academy for girls in San Antonio in 1851. The school was established on the banks of the San Antonio River at Augusta Street. In 1965 the Ursulines left the facility and moved to north San Antonio. The River Walk campus was abandoned and eventually rescued by the Conservation Society. In 1971 the grounds became home to the Southwest Craft Center, now the Southwest School of Art.

February 28, 1936 〰〰〰〰〰〰〰〰〰〰〰〰〰〰〰〰〰〰〰〰〰

As San Antonians deal with hardships of the Great Depression, chicken thieving becomes a growing concern. Law enforcement took the matter of poultry plucking seriously, and on this day the Bexar County sheriff's department pursued felony charges against three men and

Ursuline clock tower, 1961

a woman who were caught in fowl play. The forty-three chickens that were recovered were housed in the courthouse jail. The owners were contacted and asked to come in to identify the jailbirds. In the meantime the eggs that were produced were donated to charity.

MARCH

The timeline of women's history reveals a stalled though no less stalwart march toward social equity. On March 31, 1776, Abigail Adams admonished her husband, founding father John Adams, and the Continental Congress to "remember the ladies and be more generous and favorable to them than your ancestors. Do not put such unlimited power into the hands of the husbands."

She added an idea that isn't as often quoted: "Remember, all men would be tyrants if they could." She continued, saying that "if particular care and attention is not paid to the ladies, we are determined to foment a rebellion, and will not hold ourselves bound by any laws in which we have no voice or representation."

On March 27, 1934, Lydia Mendoza recorded "Mal Hombre" at Bluebird Records in San Antonio. It is a song that seems to echo Abigail Adams's assertion that "all men would be tyrants if they could." In terms of the battle of the sexes, men have always had the upper hand. The power struggle is as old as time. Mendoza sings to the "bad man" who has stolen her innocence and taken advantage of her, leaving her "abandoned," "weaker," and "defeated."

Mendoza, who began her singing career amid the chili queen stands at the Plaza del Zacate (now known as Milam Park), would become a pioneering star of the radio with regional and then national acclaim. The discrimination at hotels and restaurants she routinely faced while on tour is well documented.

Woman Suffrage Week kicked off in San Antonio on March 26, 1916. The effort was led by Eleanor Brackenridge and featured a slate of events to drum up support for the women's vote. Two years later, Gov. William P. Hobby signed the Texas suffrage bill, but it would be another two years before American women would be given the right to vote.

Smaller, quiet efforts by women emerged in the fight for equality. On March 17, 1949, it was reported that women had been admitted to Lackland Air Force Base's officer candidate school. In this "military experiment" nineteen "young and attractive" members of the Women's Air Force would be trained alongside 310 airmen in the air force's attempt to prove that men and women could work together.

On March 4, 1974, two women joined the cadet roll call at the San Antonio Police Academy. One of the women was quoted as saying that she was not moved by any women's rights efforts—she just wanted "to be treated like everyone else."

During World War II Lila Cockrell served in the WAVES branch of the U.S. Navy. In March 1970 mayor pro tem Cockrell called for a San Antonio commission on women's rights. She and other prominent women in the city sought to establish a local program that would address the issue of equal pay for equal work and provide women with education guidance and career counseling. On May 1, 1975, Cockrell became the first woman elected mayor of a major American city. She served three consecutive terms until 1981 and was elected to a fourth term in 1989 and remained in office until 1991.

World War II temporarily slowed Mendoza's burgeoning career. By that time she had recorded more than two hundred songs and was married with a family. But even in the 1970s her fame continued to spread. She was considered a folk icon and played festivals and other music venues, including on college campuses. In 1977 she sang at President Jimmy Carter's inaugural celebration. She received a National Endowment for the Arts National Heritage Award and was inducted into the Tejano Music Hall of Fame. In 2013 the U.S. Postal Service launched a music icons stamp series, and the Lydia Mendoza Forever Stamp was dedicated on May 15 in a ceremony at the Guadalupe Cultural Arts Center.

In 1999 Mendoza was awarded a National Medal of the Arts. Among the other recipients were Maria Tallchief, Rosetta LeNoire, Odetta, and Aretha Franklin, all notable women who were as outnumbered by men in their respective fields as those officer candidate students and cadets, but who dedicated their lives to their art. There isn't a tyrant or a bad man anywhere who could thwart their incomparable talents or the quiet rebellion of their assiduous efforts.

March 1, 1981 〰〰〰〰〰〰〰〰〰〰〰〰〰〰〰〰〰〰〰〰〰〰〰〰〰〰〰〰〰〰

The San Antonio Museum of Art opens to the public. The museum was christened four years earlier with the smashing of a bottle of beer rather than champagne because the grounds had been the Lone Star Brewery. The castle-like brewery was built in 1903, but Prohibition

San Antonio Museum of Art, 2015

forced its abandonment. In the 1970s Witte Museum director Jack McGregor was hunting for a house and stumbled on the dilapidated structure. Others scoffed, but he saw it as a location for the San Antonio Museum Association's collection. The property sold for $375,000, and it took $10 million to turn it into a museum.

March 2, 1835

Elected as a delegate to the Texas Independence Convention, Samuel Augustus Maverick is dispatched from the Alamo. This was the same day delegates in Washington-on-the-Brazos signed the Texas Declaration of Independence. Maverick wouldn't arrive there until March 5. As he left San Antonio, Mexican troops surrounded the Alamo and commander William Barret Travis asked him to urge the convention to send reinforcements. The next day the Alamo would be overrun. Maverick added his name to the independence document and began to help draft the Texas Constitution.

March 3, 1970

Mayor pro tem Lila Cockrell calls for a commission on women's rights in San Antonio. Cockrell, along with other prominent area women, sought to establish a local program to address gender pay equity and to provide women with education guidance and career counseling services. On May 1, 1975, Cockrell became the first woman elected mayor of a major American city and served three consecutive terms until 1981. She was elected to a fourth term on June 1, 1989, and was in office until June 1, 1991. During her tenure Cockrell guided San Antonio into the era of single-district city council seats, aquifer protection, the creation of VIA transit, and the development of the local tourism economy.

March 4, 1974

For the first time since 1959, two women join the cadet roll call at the San Antonio Police Academy to begin training as police officers. Police officials said women would be trained alongside male cadets and must meet the same strenuous standards. One of the women cadets said, "I'm not a woman liberationist. I just want to be treated like everyone else."

March 5, 1842

Mexican general Ráfael Vásquez leads his troops of about seven hundred to invade San Antonio. Republic of Texas forces were not strong enough to hold the town and evacuated without a fight after he demanded the city's surrender. Vásquez took San Antonio, raised the Mexican flag, and declared Mexican law in force. Merchant John Twohig didn't want his goods supplied to enemy forces, so he invited the poor to his store to take what they wanted. Then he blew up the building to prevent Mexican forces from getting any other remaining supplies, including gunpowder. Two days later Vásquez abandoned San Antonio and began a return march to Mexico. The invasion was regarded as a plundering, with more to follow.

March 6, 1836 〜〜〜〜〜〜〜〜〜〜〜〜〜〜〜〜〜〜〜〜〜〜〜〜〜〜〜〜〜〜〜

After being besieged for thirteen days by Mexican forces, defenders of the Alamo are overrun and defeated. Gen. Antonio López de Santa Anna, the dictator of Mexico, had declared that no defenders' lives would be spared. It's unclear how many Alamo defenders lost their lives,

Gen. Antonio López de Santa Anna, c. 1847

but the number may be as high as 257. On the Mexican side, about 600 were killed or severely wounded. The defeat at the Alamo was critical for the Texican rebellion but led to the war's victory at San Jacinto. The battle has become a symbol of patriotic sacrifice, and the story continues to be retold with varying layers of complexity.

March 7, 1836

The day after the Alamo's fall General Santa Anna orders the razing of the failed improvised fort. He may have sought to prevent the creation of a shrine for the Texican martyrs, but it's more likely that he just didn't want the structure reoccupied by Texas rebels. Santa Anna gave a direct order: he wanted not a single stone standing. That didn't happen, however. After the battle, the outer walls were already rubble, but the roofless chapel remained. Mexican soldiers may have had reservations about destroying the old mission church, and they left it standing. In 1849 the U.S. Army turned the grounds into a quartermaster depot, rebuilt the walls, and reroofed the structure—essentially creating what we recognize as the iconic Alamo today.

March 8, 1970

Otto Phillip Schnabel receives a proclamation from the city supporting his dream to make 1970 the nation's Clean-Up and Beautification Year. Known to most as O.P., the local insurance salesman was bitten by the beautification bug in 1947 when he was in Switzerland. For the next forty years Schnabel used public relations stunts and shamed city officials to bring about a fundamental change in San Antonio's culture of trash pickup and sanitation. The city won the "nation's cleanest town" contest for the next four years, from 1952 to 1955. In 1970 Schnabel sent fifty-two blinged-out push brooms to President Nixon, Vice President Agnew, and the fifty U.S. governors.

March 9, 1731

The Canary Islanders arrive at the presidio of San Antonio de Béxar with a royal decree to establish the first civilian settlement in the area. The Isleños' ship landed in Veracruz, Mexico, and they marched overland to the villa of San Fernando de Béxar. They were led by Canarian Juan Leal Goraz, who would be elected the first mayor of San Antonio. The settlers were given exclusive use of the San Pedro channel, called the Acequia Madre.

March 10, 1958

The first *Captain Gus Show* airs at 5:30 p.m. on KENS-TV. The children's program was hosted by Joe Alston—who sported a wiggly handlebar mustache, a bright orange wig, and a yachting cap—until 1979, when the show was canceled. The show format was the typical TV kiddie show with Alston introducing classic Popeye and Bugs Bunny Looney Toons cartoons. He also told corny jokes, performed silly skits, and took his handheld mic to the small audience area of bleachers on the soundstage to "meet the mateys."

March 11, 1884

Austin marshal Ben Thompson and Uvalde County sheriff King Fisher, two of the most feared pistoleros, are killed at the Vaudeville Theater in the most famous Wild West shootout in San Antonio history. The Vaudeville, at the northwest corner of Commerce and Soledad Streets, was a saloon known for being well stocked with wild women, whiskey, and ways to gamble. Thompson and Fisher walked into an ambush set by Jacob Coy and Joe Foster, who ran a card game at the establishment. Eleven days later, on March 22, Foster died of wounds from the shootout. The story made the front page of the *New York Times* and became the model of the cliché western saloon shootout. The location would be referred to as the "fatal corner" for years to come.

March 12, 1867

The San Antonio–Boerne passenger train makes its maiden voyage. With a ticket costing ninety-five cents, the locomotive took three hours to steam passengers each way. The route by stagecoach required at least seven uncomfortable hours. Furthermore, ferrying goods demanded an oxcart and a full day. The rail connection essentially saved Boerne, founded eighteen years earlier with the name Tusculum. The remote village was falling short in attracting new residents, but the arrival of the iron horse changed that.

March 13, 1939

Students at Thomas Edison High School walk out of class carrying signs that read, "We want a gym." Some four hundred marched for three hours in outrage over the failure of a school bond election. That afternoon the Los Angeles Heights Independent School District board promised students they would try to find a way to build the gym. The bond sought $75,000, which would have been matched with Works Progress Administration funds. The Los Angeles Heights district merged with San Antonio Independent School District in 1949, and in 1958 Edison High School moved to a new campus complete with a gym.

March 14, 1941

Maury Maverick announces his campaign for reelection for mayor, setting up one of the bitterest election fights in city history. Promising reform, Maverick had been elected mayor two years earlier. The previous mayor, C. K. Quin, who had an association with the Ku Klux Klan, enjoyed ties to the city's saloons, gambling houses, and brothels. Quin was indicted in 1938 for misusing city funds to buy votes. He blamed Maverick for the indictment and entered the race to settle the score. Seeking to undo Maverick's reforms, many local officials rallied behind Quin, including Sheriff Owen Kilday. Quin defeated Maverick by about a thousand votes.

March 15, 1967 〰〰〰〰〰〰〰〰〰〰〰〰〰〰〰〰〰〰〰〰〰〰〰〰〰〰〰

Amid a shower of boos and hisses, the Bexar County Commissioners Court doubles the taxes for the Bexar County Hospital District. The vote was three to two, with county judge Blair Reeves breaking the tie. The tax increase was adopted despite a January 14 referendum on the issue that voters overwhelmingly rejected. It was necessary to fund a medical school and teaching hospital in San Antonio. In 1961 Bexar County voters approved a bond issue that included $5 million for construction of a three-hundred-bed hospital that would also be a teaching facility for physicians in training. But the tax increase was needed for the hospital's operations. In September 1968 the University of Texas Medical School at San Antonio opened its doors and began accepting students. Two months later the Bexar County teaching hospital began admitting patients.

March 16, 1960

San Antonio integrates its lunch counters. The NAACP planned a "day of action" with sit-ins and pickets to protest the city's Jim Crow practice of prohibiting African Americans from being served at downtown lunch counters. San Antonio police told restaurant owners they would not break up the peaceful protests. The restaurateurs then announced that they would drop the Jim Crow barrier. In front of reporters and photographers, four African Americans dined at the Woolworth's lunch counter. The event didn't occur unmarred, however, as the same day two large wooden crosses were discovered in Travis Park next to the Confederate soldiers' monument. The crosses were wrapped in kerosene-soaked rags, and one was ablaze. A threatening letter from the Ku Klux Klan that warned "Beware you Black People" was also found.

March 17, 1949

Women join the ranks of Lackland Air Force Base officer candidate school. In an experiment to ascertain the viability of coeducation at the officer candidate school, nineteen "young and attractive" women received training alongside 310 trouser-wearing airmen. The air force was attempting to prove that men and women can work alongside each other without issues. According to the *San Antonio Light*, this was the first time the U.S. military had gone coed. The only possible problem was that the

Officer candidate, Lackland Air Force Base, 1952

women candidates were performing too well and had "set a standard of perfection on and off the field." One commanding officer was quoted as saying, "You'd be surprised what the presence of three or four women in a classroom does. It raises the whole class spirit. I think the men in the group are surprising themselves. They have to work at least three times as hard to keep up with the women."

March 18, 1912

A locomotive explodes outside the Southern Pacific roundhouse on North Hackberry Street, leaving thirty people dead and dozens more injured. Locomotive 704 had built up a head of pressurized steam when safety valves failed and the eruption shot iron shrapnel a mile in every direction. The concussive blast damaged buildings just as far. Lawsuits against the railroad were filed immediately, and all cases were settled out of court. The roundhouse disaster was one of the worst boiler explosions in the history of rail.

March 19, 1840

The deadly clash between San Antonio settlers and the Comanche emerges as the "Council House Fight." What happened remains controversial even today. Comanche representatives came to San Antonio looking to trade captives for peace. Their prisoners were several Mexican children and sixteen-year-old Matilda Lockhart, who had clearly been tortured and mutilated. When talks broke down and the Comanche attempted to leave, the shooting started. Thirty Comanche leaders and warriors and five tribal women and children were killed by San Antonio soldiers and citizens in a battle waged in the dirt streets of the frontier village.

March 20, 1939 //

City officials push back at statements made by First Lady Eleanor Roosevelt about conditions in San Antonio. Roosevelt had visited the city several days earlier, and her comments were published in her nationally syndicated column "My Day." She wrote about the terrible conditions in the city for the "Latin American citizens," saying, "Sad as it may seem, San Antonio has the highest tuberculosis rate in the country and it is not far behind in social disease." Mayor C. K. Quin said Roosevelt's facts were "incorrect" and complained that the column was bad publicity for the city. Roosevelt also wrote about the city's need for public housing: "There is a housing program of some size which will make a great difference in the living conditions of the Latin American citizens when it is actually finished, but it has not as yet begun. I am told that there is some opposition, but after driving through the district and going into some of the houses, I can only feel that out of purely selfish interest all opposition will disappear, for a district which breeds disease and shelters crime is harmful to the whole community."

March 21, 1845

New Braunfels is founded north of San Antonio at the point where the Comal and Guadalupe Rivers meet. New Braunfels was the first Texas colony of German immigrants established by Prince Carl of Solms-Braunfels. During their first spring the new arrivals erected a fort, divided land, and began building their homes. By the summer their numbers had reached just under four hundred. The German community thrived and began to influence San Antonio. In the 1850s it was not uncommon to hear German spoken in the streets and shops of San Antonio. The city was seen as having three distinct languages— Spanish, English, and German.

March 22, 1969

San Antonio leaders are warned of hippies providing youth with drugs and Communist propaganda. A Bexar County district attorney investigator testified before the Texas Senate Youth Affairs Subcommittee hearing on juvenile crime, held at Saint Mary's University, and told of a hippie haven downtown where illegal narcotics and sex were easily available, along with Communist literature provided by "pacifists" and "drug pushers."

March 23, 1906

Lucille LeSueur, who will later become known as Joan Crawford, is born in San Antonio. Crawford arrived in San Antonio in poverty and unwanted. Her father deserted the family before she was born. The LeSueurs lived on South Cherry Street in what she called a "drab little rented house on the wrong side of the tracks." She didn't stay there long. Her mother moved with a new husband to Lawton, Oklahoma. Later Crawford became a showgirl dancing in traveling revues. She was determined to become a Hollywood star and let nothing stand in her way. In 1945 she won an Oscar for best actress for her role in the film *Mildred Pierce*.

March 24, 1938

The city council approves San Antonio's zoning ordinance, eighteen months in the making. City hall began developing a zoning plan in November 1936. At the time San Antonio and Houston were the only two major U.S. cities without a zoning ordinance. The plan divided the city into thirteen districts and thirty-two zones and regulated building height, lot size, and building use. The council said the ordinance was needed to keep objectionable types of structures and industries out of certain parts of the city, but it was also aimed at maintaining San Antonio's segregation by race, class, and ethnicity.

March 25, 1941

Robert Emmet Lucey arrives in San Antonio and is installed two days later as archbishop. He announced that the social betterment of the city would be his chief aim: "All of my efforts, in addition to performing my regular ecclesiastical duties, will be directed toward carrying on the social work of the late Archbishop Arthur Jerome Drossaerts." Drossaerts, San Antonio's first archbishop, served from 1918 until his death in 1940 and was best known for providing refuge to clergy who fled persecution during the anti-Catholic hysteria of the Mexican Revolution. Lucey transformed the local Catholic Church with implementation of the Catholic Welfare Bureau, the Catholic Action Office, and other initiatives aimed at helping the needy, sick, and destitute. He earned a national reputation as a champion of civil rights and social justice and integrated local parochial schools before the 1954 *Brown v. Board of Education* Supreme Court decision. He was an outspoken defender of the war in Vietnam. His last years as archbishop were troubled by a virtual revolt by younger priests over their involvement in politics. On July 4, 1969, Lucey was forced to retire at age seventy-eight. He was replaced by Archbishop Francis J. Furey.

March 26, 1916

Woman Suffrage Week kicks off in the Alamo City. The Equal Franchise Society planned events for each evening that week to drum up support for recognizing the women's vote. Led by Eleanor Brackenridge, San Antonio was blazing the Texas trail in the fight for gender equality at the polls. It paid off two years later, on March 26, 1918, when Gov. William P. Hobby signed the Texas suffrage bill. It would be 1920, however, before the Nineteenth Amendment would be ratified, guaranteeing American women the right to vote.

March 27, 1934

Lydia Mendoza records the song "Mal Hombre." Known as "La Alondra de la Frontera" or the "Lark of the Border," Mendoza was a Latina pioneering star of radio. She started out singing with her sisters in San Antonio amid the chili queen stands at the Plaza del Zacate. In 1934 she composed "Mal Hombre" for Bluebird Records in San Antonio, and it became a hit with Spanish-speaking audiences. Mendoza became a regional and national radio star, but on tour she routinely faced discrimination at hotels and restaurants that refused to serve Mexican Americans. In 1999 she was awarded the National Medal of Arts.

March 28, 1935

The Dust Bowl comes to San Antonio. For two days a dust storm battered south-central Texas, delivering a sheet of black dirt, lowering visibility, and dropping temperatures some ten degrees. The worst of the "Dirty Thirties" was about to hit Texas and Oklahoma. The term "Dust Bowl" wouldn't be coined for another month, on April 14, when the Black Blizzard hit the Panhandle. It wasn't known at the time that this was a man-made environmental disaster, mitigated when the federal government began to require soil conservation and better land management.

March 29, 1813

At the confluence of Rosillo and Salado Creeks in southern Bexar County, forces of Spanish Royalists clash with the Republican Army of the North in the Battle of Rosillo. This was mainly an American filibuster expedition led by José Bernardo Gutiérrez de Lara and Samuel Kemper. After the Americans' victory at Rosillo, the Spanish governor surrendered San Antonio. He was executed, and the first Republic of Texas was declared. That republic came to a quick end, however, when Spanish forces crushed the Republican Army of the North on August 18 at the Battle of Medina, followed by bloody reprisals against the Texas rebels and the people of San Antonio.

March 30, 1924

Alamo Heights appoints a town marshal to halt the destruction of wildflowers. Town inhabitants were up in arms over what they called ruthless vandals destroying fields of laurels and bluebonnets. The Alamo Heights city council enacted an ordinance protecting the wild-flowers, and Paul Villaret was named wildflower marshal. Violators could be fined up to $100. Mayor Robert O'Grady blamed the problem on thieves who ripped out bluebonnets by the roots and chopped laurel blooms off trees. He said they hauled the flora to town to decorate places of business.

March 31, 1995

Selena Quintanilla-Pérez is fatally shot in Corpus Christi by Yolanda Saldívar, her first fan club founder and manager of Selena Etc. The death shocked San Antonio fans, who adored and admired Selena for her Tejano music, fashion sense, and personal agency. The Grammy-winning singer was poised for crossover success into pop stardom. San Antonio radio stations began playing Selena music tribute marathons, and local television stations produced specials about her rise. The *New York Times* covered the singer's death with a front-page story, and reaction to her death was a watershed event for national media, which for the first time witnessed the potential of the Latino market. Gov. George W. Bush proclaimed April 16, 1995, Selena Day. Selena's family founded the Selena Foundation. Her bilingual album *Dreaming of You*, released posthumously in 1995, was the first Tejano album to hit number one in the United States.

The story goes that Rosie Castro's mother won $300 in a menudo cook-off at Market Square. San Antonian Rosie Castro—known for her civil rights activism—went into labor and gave birth to twin boys on September 16, 1974. The menudo money was used to help pay the hospital bills.

Abraham Lincoln was born in a log cabin. Lots of people were born in log cabins in the early 1800s, but the detail has become part of his origin story. Calvin Coolidge was born on the Fourth of July. George Washington did not chop down a cherry tree. He did, however, throw a piece of slate into the Rappahannock River in his boyhood home of Fredericksburg, Virginia. That ordinary detail is somehow more compelling than the mythical anecdote about his contrition and honesty, perhaps meant to influence young children, trotted out repeatedly for generations as part of parents' admonitions to their kids to eat their peas and stay out of trouble.

Joaquín and Julián Castro have quite the trifecta of origin stories as politicians and public servants. They are the sons of a civil rights activist, they were born on Diez y Seis de Septiembre, and the hospital bill was paid for with prize money for the best menudo in San Antonio.

That must have been some really good menudo— though the soup's appeal is lost on plenty of folks who turn up their noses at beef tripe (in the Mexican recipe), hominy, or both. Long known as a home remedy for a hangover, the dish remains a restaurant staple for patrons hunched over a brimming bowl on Sunday mornings, black coffee eschewed for the broth and its zesty promise of quick recovery.

Perhaps menudo has not enjoyed the recent popularity of tamales or variations on the basic Mexican recipe. While the majority of San Antonians won't deviate from their abuelita's tamal recipe, gourmet versions that feature goat cheese or some other ingredient not found in a South Side cocina can still be delectable. Still, no matter what trending comestible ends up in the sweet or savory dish, spicy pork or bean tamales remain the gold standard to measure all other tamales by.

It stands to reason that the way to wow a presidential candidate in the Alamo City is to serve him a plate of tamales. Unfortunately no one could have predicted in 1976 that President Gerald Ford wouldn't remove the corn husk before putting the tamal to his lips. About what has become known in the media as the "Great Tamales Incident," Mayor Lila Cockrell surmised that Ford simply "didn't get a briefing on the eating of tamales."

Tamales have been part of this country's cuisine since at least 1848, and their history in this part of the world dates to 8,000 to 5,000 BC. They were served at Aztec banquets and eaten in homes even before the conquest of Spain. In spite of that history, in 1976 they were still exotic to some people from other parts of the United

States. Taken in the most troubling light, the "Great Tamales Incident" speaks to the yawning chasm that separates us, the lack of comprehension about the cultures of people who have always made up this country.

The ubiquity of the Mexican version of the tamal in San Antonio gives its denizens no excuse to gag on the inedible, striated corn *oja* or husk. Legions of industrious women (and men) make and sell them by the dozens upon countless dozens, including meatless and vegan versions, with raisins or without, jalapeños or not, around the November and December holidays and well into the new year. Sugary sweet versions are sold at Easter time.

Today's so-called foodie culture—for good or ill—closes the wide gap of comprehension about tamales and the culture from which they came, but it does so with a Food Network basket of mystery ingredients far more than it celebrates the original tamal. One thing is certain: whether the tamal is traditional or features an unfamiliar delicacy, all we have to do is remove that thick, unforgiving, crenellated shell to try to see what's underneath.

April 1, 1936

An April Fool's joke in the *San Antonio Light* may have hit a nerve with readers. A story reported that patriotic San Antonians' vigilance was all that saved the historic

Alamo from being stolen from the city. Since Dallas was awarded the state's centennial celebration, its citizens had been casting envious eyes on San Antonio to see what else they could misappropriate. Then they remembered the Alamo. Early risers who were at Alamo Plaza spotted workers loading the Alamo onto the back of a truck to be taken to Dallas for an exhibition at the centennial. Irate citizens were able to summon the police and restore the Shrine of Texas Liberty to its proper place.

April 2, 1849

The cholera epidemic begins. The 1849 mass infection was the worst outbreak San Antonians had ever witnessed. It lasted six weeks and killed at least six hundred from a population of five thousand. The lack of a hospital was a factor in the high death rate. The Sisters of Charity of the Incarnate Word would remedy that, and on December 1, 1869, they opened the Santa Rosa Infirmary. It has grown into today's Christus Santa Rosa Health System.

April 3, 1917

War fever hits San Antonio, and the city declares a general holiday for the celebration of Loyalty Day. Three days before the United States entered World War I, the Alamo City was bedecked with red, white, and blue in what was called "the biggest outburst of patriotism ever witnessed in a southern city." Thousands of men, women, and children lined Houston and Commerce Streets for a parade of marching bands, military troops, and labor organizations. The celebrants could not anticipate the savage horrors that would be unleashed in the world's first industrialized war.

April 4, 1719

The Aguayo expedition reaches San Antonio. The French invasion of East Texas had forced a Spanish retreat, and Marqués de Aguayo was commissioned to reoccupy the area. Some members of the expedition remained while the force's main body proceeded. In 1721 some members of the expedition returned to San Antonio to establish a third mission and rebuild the Béxar presidio. The expedition established eight missions across Texas and solidified Spain's claim to the land.

April 5, 1950

Two air force pilots chase a bright object in the sky from Austin to San Antonio. At 1:45 p.m. fighter pilots were scrambled from Bergstrom Air Force Base and ordered into the air. The two pilots climbed to forty thousand feet in pursuit of the unidentified flying object and kept the bogey in sight for thirty minutes. They reported that the object didn't seem to be an aircraft or any flying machine, and after reaching San Antonio they broke off the chase. They concluded that they were probably chasing a planet; it was likely Venus.

April 6, 1971

The Committee for Barrio Betterment loses in a landslide to the Good Government League for city council. The committee ticket was composed of Willie Benavides, Mario Compean, Gloria Cabrera, and Rosie Castro. Fueled by fears that Crystal City's La Raza Unida political wave would reach San Antonio, voter turnout hit 52 percent, and the Good Government League ticket easily won. But this was the league's swan song; local Latino politics was now in force and the league would never again win control of city hall. Castro and company didn't win, but she called the results a victory and the campaign changed San Antonio politics. Benavides told supporters, "We'll be back."

April 7, 1966

The Toudouze family is forced to evacuate their home at 123 Wyoming Street to make way for HemisFair. As bulldozers prepared to demolish their home, Frank Toudouze played "May the Good Lord Bless and Keep You" on his harmonica. He said the song was dedicated to the "good people." His seventy-five-year-old mother wept as sheriff deputies broke the door locks to evict the family from their condemned dwelling. Court-appointed commissioners offered $9,800 for the Toudouze home, and a writ of possession was ordered. Then came a court battle to save the homestead. Toudouze insisted that the process was not legal and his neighborhood was not a "slum area."

April 8, 1951

Joe W. Thiele, chair of the San Antonio Chamber of Commerce national promotion committee, announces his bold prediction concerning the city's future. Speaking at Trinity University, Thiele lectured on the city's prospects and said it would continue its extraordinary growth. He said the city would be home to more than seven hundred thousand residents in 1970—population 723,182, to be exact. According to the U.S. Census Bureau, the population in 1950 was 408,442; in 1970 it was 654,153, which was still impressive. In 1950 San Antonio was ranked the twenty-fifth-largest city in the country, and in 1970 it was ranked fifteenth. Thiele claimed that he coined the slogan "San Antonio, America's fastest growing major city." In 2018 the population was pegged at 1,511,946, and the city was ranked seventh largest in the country.

April 9, 1976

President Gerald Ford visits San Antonio in his presidential election campaign and is given a plate of tamales.

He picked one up and bit into it without removing the corn husk, and the Great Tamal Incident was born. Veteran CBS correspondent Bob Schieffer recalls that Ford "nearly choked." Mike Huckabee, a former Republican presidential candidate, said the blunder became a media focal point, as Texans found it too hard to swallow that Ford had fumbled the tamal test. Huckabee said it cost him Texas. Democrat Jimmy Carter won the White House.

April 10, 1939

The first issue of the *San Antonio Register* is published. Focusing on issues important to African Americans, the weekly newspaper ran for forty-seven years without interruption. Charles Bellinger, the city's black political boss, founded the paper when the *San Antonio Inquirer* refused to publish his political ad. Three years later the *Inquirer* folded. The *Register*, which was circulated widely across the South, reported on the lynchings and other horrors of Jim Crow violence that were routinely ignored by the mainstream newspapers.

April 11, 1917

The U.S. Senate authorizes the purchase of 1,200 acres to the northeast of Fort Sam Houston to expand the base. Some senators balked at the $330,000 price, but Sen. James Wadsworth Jr. of New York explained

Charles Bellinger, c. 1930

that "San Antonio will always be an exceedingly important concentration point for American troops. If it ever becomes necessary for the government to send troops to Mexico, these troops will be assembled at San Antonio."

April 12, 1793

Mission San Antonio de Valero is secularized, and the land and livestock are surrendered by the Catholic Church. Under Spanish rule, administrative *justicias* were appointed to divide mission property with the intention of protecting the best interests of the indigenous people. It would be thirty years before the other four San Antonio missions were secularized. Soon after San Antonio de Valero closed, the Second Flying Company of San Carlos de Parras, a company of mounted Spanish lancers, arrived and established it as a fort. They were likely the first to call the complex the Alamo.

April 13, 1709

A Spanish expedition reaches the site that is now San Antonio and comes upon a natural artesian well. The expedition was led by Father Antonio de San Buenaventura y Olivares and accompanied by Father Isidro Félix de Espinosa, who wrote that "after going through a mesquite flat and some oak groves we came to an irrigation ditch, bordered by many trees and with enough water to supply a town." Since it was the feast day of Saint Peter, they named it San Pedro Springs.

April 14, 1930 //

A controversy erupts over a proposal to extend Fredericksburg Road at Five Points to San Pedro Avenue. Five Points is where Fredericksburg converges with Flores, West Laurel, North Cameron, and North Laredo Streets, making for one of the city's most congested intersections at the time. Opponents complained that it would make the traffic even worse, but there was enthusiasm for improving access to the expanding Woodlawn Hills neighborhood, and land to build the road was donated to the city by District Builders. The plan, which was approved some two months later, was hailed as the greatest city improvement of 1930.

April 15, 1938 //

Police chief Owen Kilday and a squad of handpicked officers raid an alleged "school for communism" at 3007 West Commerce Street, seizing literature and Communist writings. Officials said the school was teaching Communist subjects in English, Spanish, and Russian. Labor organizer Emma Tenayuca was arrested in the roundup with other local union officials and peace activists. Cassie Jane Winfree, state labor chair for the Women's

International League for Peace and Freedom, told police she had been informed that the school was "to educate labor leaders to organize agriculture workers."

April 16, 1852

San Antonio passes its first ordinance targeting slaves—a curfew ordering them in their homes by 9:30 p.m. Those caught in the street after the curfew bell rang would be apprehended and kept in the "calaboose" until the master paid a $5 fine. Alternatively slaves could work the fine off in servitude to the city or pay by being whipped. The ordinance was later amended to prohibit slaves from selling items, carrying weapons, and possessing alcohol.

April 17, 1776

María Josefa Granados marries Fernando Veramendi. Granados, age seventeen, was a descendant of the first conquerors and rulers of the Canary Islands, and her family was held in high regard in San Fernando de Béxar society. The thirty-three-year-old Veramendi was a merchant. The blessed union created a social and economic powerhouse that aided in establishing San Antonio as a center of commerce in the frontier. In 1783 Veramendi was killed by Apaches while on a trip to Mexico City. The widowed Doña María Josefa continued to operate the largest general store in San Antonio.

April 18, 1842

Juan Seguín resigns as mayor. Born in San Antonio to a prominent family, Seguín fought in the Texas Revolution and escaped death at the Alamo when he was sent out as a courier. Seguín was elected to the Republic of Texas senate. He was also elected mayor of San Antonio, but his time in office was controversial. Anglo squatters on city property spread rumors accusing him of betraying Texas to Mexico. Fearing for his life, Seguín resigned and fled with his family to Mexico. He fought against the invading United States in the Mexican War.

April 19, 1957

San Antonio oilman and adventurer Tom Slick is quoted as saying that his exploring party in the Himalayas found three sets of mysterious tracks, which he is convinced were made by the fabled "abominable snowman." Slick was active in cryptozoology and sought to prove the existence of Bigfoot, the Yeti, and the Loch Ness Monster. Slick founded several legitimate research organizations, including Texas Biomedical Research Institute, the Southwest Research Institute, and the Mind Science Foundation. He was an advocate for global harmony, and his legacy continues to fund scholarship in world peace.

April 20, 1923

In a fiery tragedy at Fiesta, two firefighters are killed and eleven injured when an eighty-two-foot-tall bonfire prematurely ignites. The firefighters had planned to stage an exhibition of their rescue skills as a fundraiser, and the wooden structure was stuffed with hay and soaked with gasoline. It was to be the highlight of the 1923 Fiesta. When the rescue dummy fell from the top platform, two firefighters climbed the structure to set it upright and the tower caught fire.

April 21, 1887

The ancient Greek play *Damon and Pythias* is staged by a company of local amateur thespians. Staged at the Grand Opera House with multiple evening performances, the play earned a rave review in the *San Antonio Daily Express*: "It can safely be asserted it is one of the best amateur productions of so heavy of caliber that has been placed on the boards." The reviewer praised W. G. Tobin's performance in the role of Damon and called him a "distinctive and historic talent." John W. Tobin was praised for his acting grace in the role of Procles. The paper wasn't so kind to the third Tobin on stage, however: "Mr. Chas W. Tobin would do better as Lucilius if he had a lot less self-consciousness."

April 22, 1976

Secretary of Defense Donald Rumsfeld says the "fate was sealed months ago" for cutbacks at Kelly Air Force Base but offers the twelve hundred workers his sympathies. He was on a whirlwind tour of the Lackland facilities and Kelly's C5 jumbo jet maintenance program. Kelly was closed in 1995 when the Base Realignment and Closure Commission decided the base should be realigned with Lackland and its workload consolidated with that of other air force depots. On July 13, 2001, Kelly was decommissioned and became KellyUSA. Later that year the air force transferred more than a thousand acres of the former base to Port San Antonio.

April 23, 1861

U.S. Army officers from the Eighth U.S. Infantry stationed in San Antonio are seized as prisoners of war. It was the early days of the Civil War, and the Confederacy had attacked Fort Sumter two weeks earlier. Union officers were quickly offered pardons, which they accepted under protest. After signing documents and pledging not to do harm to the Confederacy, the officers were allowed to go home. But first, two soldiers secretly took the regimental and American flags that had been carried in the Mexican War and returned them to Washington, D.C.

April 24, 1891

The first Battle of Flowers parade takes place. The parade, meant to celebrate the anniversary of the victory at San Jacinto, was scheduled to coincide with President Benjamin Harrison's visit, but rain forced a four-day delay. Then with clear skies, but without Harrison, the parade went on. At its conclusion, women celebrated by throwing flowers at each other. On April 24, 1948, the first Fiesta Flambeau Parade was held, but in its debut it was called simply the Fiesta Night Illuminated Parade.

April 25, 1885

At an annual shooting contest at San Pedro Springs, the marksmanship of San Antonio's newspaper reporters are put on display. Each contestant was issued ten glass balls for targets. Of the six entries, *Light* reporter M. H. Claytor had the truest aim and was rewarded with the prize of a shotgun presented by the Alamo Gun Club. There were no injuries except for one reporter's dental filling, which was knocked out of his mouth by the gun's recoil.

April 26, 1914

More than fifty San Antonians of Mexican descent send a telegram to President Woodrow Wilson offering their services if war breaks out with Mexico. A spokesperson said more than a hundred Texas Mexicans were ready to shoulder a military rifle should the occasion require. Relations between the United States and Mexico were at the breaking point, and the Tampico Affair nearly triggered a full war. Earlier that month the U.S. Navy had shelled and occupied the city of Veracruz. While some in the United States called for a full occupation of Mexico, Wilson limited the invasion to Veracruz.

April 27, 1979

A sniper attacks spectators at the Battle of Flowers parade. Ira Attebury parked his motor home along the parade route at East Grayson Street and Broadway and fired into the crowd for thirty minutes. Attebury, age sixty-four, suffered from paranoia and had a hoard of weapons in his trailer. Two women died and seventeen people suffered serious wounds, including five police officers. After a gun battle with police, Attebury died from a self-inflicted gunshot to the head. Were it not for a police officer who bravely drove his police car in front of Attebury's field of vision, the tragedy would have been much worse.

April 28, 1966

The city council votes to approve the purchase of 640 acres near the municipal airport for a park. The land cost $613,652 and the funds were from the 1964 bond issue. Originally called the Northeast Preserve, the park opened on April 13, 1968, with public trails and picnic areas. In June 1974 it was renamed McAllister Park in honor of former mayor Walter W. McAllister. More acreage has been added, and the park is now 976 acres.

April 29, 1872

The old central dome of San Fernando Cathedral collapses. The center of pride, faith, and community in the city's earliest days, the church was in a ruinous state by 1840. One observer noted that half of the roof was gone and swallows and bats flew about inside. An extensive renovation was planned in 1851, but it did not start until 1868. Under the direction of architect François Giraud, the original bell tower and part of the nave were razed. Giraud's design included a Gothic Revival nave, triple entrance portals, a gable roof, and twin bell towers and buttresses. By 1873 the old dirt floor and most of the limestone rubble walls mortared with goat milk were gone, and in October of that year the new church was consecrated. The second bell tower was completed in 1902.

April 30, 1976

Two future presidents barnstorm San Antonio. Republican Ronald Reagan was challenging President Gerald Ford for the party's nomination. Warning of bloodshed of whites in Africa, Reagan delivered a fiery speech at the Alamo, blasting Ford's support of black majority rule in Rhodesia (now Zimbabwe). This racist rhetoric found a receptive audience and rejuvenated Reagan's failing campaign. Hours later, Georgia governor Jimmy Carter, who was leading in the race for the Democratic nomination, was in San Antonio. He promised cuts to the nation's military spending and said he wouldn't promise

San Fernando Cathedral, 2018

to protect the city's military bases. Carter won the presidency. Reagan won the Texas GOP primary, defeating
Ford in all twenty-four congressional districts, and took
all ninety-six delegates at stake in the state's first binding
primary. Four years later he won the presidency.

MAY

In Tomás Rivera's seminal book *And the Earth Did Not Devour Him*, Marcos comes of age facing a number of impossible tests. His brother Julián is missing in action in Korea, and the family must leave South Texas and travel north to pick crops in order to survive the worst of their poverty. In Minnesota, Marcos goes head to head with the forces of racism and discrimination. His father and siblings come close to death working in the fields. He watches several family friends succumb to the ravages of deplorable working conditions.

These and other episodes cause Marcos to doubt his faith. In the deepest part of an anxious night, Marcos goes to the backyard of his family home and attempts to summon the devil. Nothing happens, and Marcos responds with fear and apprehension; it is as if the devil himself had appeared there and done his worst to the adolescent boy. To Marcos's mind, if there is no devil, there is no God. And yet he is confronted daily with what he deems as punishing malevolent and immoral forces.

The problem of evil is one that perplexes believers and nonbelievers, the clergy and the laity, the religious and the secular. The citizens of San Antonio have collectively endured the pall of evil in their midst over the past three centuries. In May 2017 Genene Jones was charged in the 1981 death of an infant; Jones, who served as a pediatric nurse in the 1970s and 1980s, is suspected of killing as many as sixty children during her time working. It is believed that she committed the murders to position herself as a hero.

The Jones case is the stuff of movies. It's hard to believe that it could have happened in San Antonio.

Cheers sitcom star Woody Harrelson is often evoked in discussions about the 1979 murder of district judge John H. Wood Jr. at the hands of Harrelson's father, Charles, who was a professional hitman. The elder Harrelson was allegedly hired for $250,000 by Jamiel "Jimmy" Chagra, a drug kingpin who was set to face trial in Wood's courtroom. Harrelson was convicted in 1982 and sentenced to two consecutive life terms plus five years. He was found dead in his jail cell in 2007, the cause believed to be a heart attack.

The younger Harrelson has borne this dubious mark of association to his father for his entire adult life. "The sins of the father are to be laid upon the children," wrote William Shakespeare in *The Merchant of Venice*. In a thriving, complicated city, perhaps all children are burdened with that heavy load.

The Heidi Search Center, which opened on August 4, 1990, was established after eleven-year-old Heidi Seeman was abducted from her neighborhood in northeast San Antonio while walking home from a sleepover at a friend's house. Her father led a search that grew exponentially from a small group of friends and family to thousands from the city and surrounding communities. Mayor Lila Cockrell declared August 11, 1990, Find Heidi Day, and it's believed that three hundred thousand citizens participated in the search that day.

It's believed that there has never been a search party as big as the one for Heidi. Some eight thousand volunteers searched every day for three weeks, covering twelve hundred miles. It's reported that volunteers used fifty miles of yellow ribbon to wrap around trees and on buildings throughout the city.

Around the same time, seven-year-old Erica Marie Botello was abducted from the playground outside her apartment complex in southwest San Antonio. Members of the newly established Heidi Search Center were alerted and went in search of clues about the little girl.

Both girls were eventually found murdered. Heidi's body was found in Wimberley, Texas, and Erica's was discovered in a storm drain one mile from her home.

The center closed its doors in 2018 after thirty years of service to the community through education and advocacy. Heidi, smiling back from the posters that blanketed the city during her search, did much to create something positive out of something horrific.

Bad things do happen to good people. Terrible things happen in cities. The free will and personal choice every human possesses bring tremendous potential for dire consequences.

In Rivera's book, Bartolo is a wandering poet, a historian and a philosopher of sorts, who sings songs about the citizens of the town. One of his lessons to Marcos is that he should read poems out loud because the "voice is the seed of love in the darkness."

Marcos comes of age as he faces the loss of his brother in the war, his family's extreme privation, and the terrible things he witnesses in the migrant fields. He is, we come to understand, the alter ego of Rivera, whose novel is the voice to which Bartolo refers.

There are no photos of Marcos's brother, not a whisper of his voice. What remains is Marcos and his own voice to continue to tell the stories of those who have been lost, so that others will always remember.

May 1, 1972

A panel of environmentalists urges the city to purchase one hundred square miles of the Edwards Aquifer recharge zone, in the northern part of Bexar County, for $70 million. The purchase would protect the city's water supply from pollution caused by further development. The area was sparsely populated at the time, and the concern was that by the end of the century it would see urban sprawl that would damage the environment. Authors of a study behind the proposal said the purchase was feasible and practical and that city, state, and federal funds could be found for the deal. The plea was ignored.

May 2, 1940

San Antonio expands. Since the city's founding, the map of the city had been perfectly square, with the center point being the top of the San Fernando Cathedral dome. In May 1940 that square was six miles each way, but this first set of city annexations broke the boundary into an irregular shape to the northwest and southeast. Seven new areas were added, including Los Angeles Heights, Jefferson Manor, Olmos Terrace, and Harlandale. By 2014 San Antonio's footprint had swelled by 497 square miles.

May 3, 1980

The San Antonio Botanical Garden officially opens to the public with the explicit mission to inspire visitors to connect with the world of plants and understand their importance in our lives. In 1877 the San Antonio Water Works, eventually owned by George Brackenridge, was using a former limestone quarry near the eastern end of what became Mahncke Park as its reservoir. Some one hundred years later the botanical gardens adapted the space as an amphitheater. In 1899 Brackenridge deeded the land to the city, and in 1970 voters approved $250,000 in bonds for the garden project. With additional funding from the Ewing Halsell Foundation and others, the dream of a garden showplace took root and bloomed.

May 4, 1991

San Antonio voters say no to Applewhite. City leaders had long searched for a surface water supply that could supplement the Edwards Aquifer. In 1979 the city planning commission recommended a project that would become known as the Applewhite Reservoir. It would take a decade to obtain the federal and state permits to begin building the artificial lake. A site was chosen along a seven-mile stretch of the Medina River, and initial work began in 1981. The reservoir, however, was opposed by water advocates like Fay Sinkin, who feared it was a scheme that would eventually allow greater development over the recharge zone. She called for greater protection of the aquifer and water conservation instead of the construction of a wasteful reservoir. A petition drive brought the issue to the voters. Applewhite supporters were the city's establishment and claimed that the reservoir was necessary for the city's future. In 1994 Applewhite returned to the voters, and they again said no.

May 5, 1718

The Villa de Béxar is founded after the Marqués de Valero, the viceroy of New Spain, directed governor Don Martín de Alarcón to establish a settlement on the San Antonio River. This would be the center of Spanish defense in the Texas territory and the first civilian presence

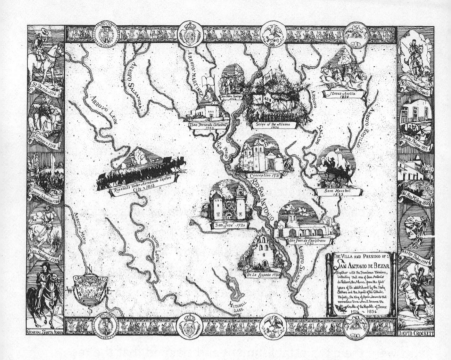

in Texas. The outpost was named in honor of the Duque de Béxar, the viceroy's brother, who died in a Spanish military campaign against the Turks near Budapest. The mission established near the presidio was named after the viceroy. Mission San Antonio de Valero later became known as the Alamo.

May 6, 2000

San Antonio voters reject a $1.5 billion light-rail proposal that would have crisscrossed the city with fifty-four miles of rail lines and promised to get residents out of their traffic-jammed cars. To pay for it required a quarter-cent increase in the sales tax. The proposal was so soundly rejected, with 70 percent of voters against it, that the city remains one of the country's largest without light-rail. The pro-rail campaign was poorly communicated, and the opposition was vocal and well-funded. Subsequent efforts to resurrect light-rail have also failed to find support. Four of the five proposals on the ballot that day, referred to as Mayor Howard Peak's Better Future agenda, failed, including the ones to do with light-rail, the redevelopment of Kelly Air Force Base, the River Walk extension, and an economic development proposal. Only a $65 million plan to protect the city's watershed and build new parks passed.

May 7, 2008 〰〰〰〰〰〰〰〰〰〰〰〰〰〰〰〰〰〰〰〰〰〰〰〰〰〰〰〰〰〰〰〰〰〰〰〰

The day after a devastating fire, San Antonio's Catholic leaders and community vow to rebuild Our Lady of the Lake University. The four-alarm blaze gutted the university's Gothic Main Building and administrative offices. The school was founded in 1895 by the Sisters of the Congregation of Divine Providence to bring education and service to San Antonio's West Side. In 1919 the institution was admitted into the Texas Association of Colleges. A decade after the fire, enrollment has climbed and academic programs have been added. The rebuilt

Main Building has been modernized, and its iconic profile continues to enhance the San Antonio skyline.

May 8, 1941

Dueling campaign rallies are held as the city prepares to vote in a dramatic rematch for mayor. Maury Maverick was looking for his first reelection victory, but C. K. Quin wanted voters to put him back in the mayor's office. In the Los Angeles Heights neighborhood Quin featured a cowboy and cowgirl band with tap dancers to attract a crowd of two thousand. Sheriff Owen Kilday joined Quin on stage and delivered a full-throated endorsement of the anti-Maverick ticket. Maverick called Quin's tactics and promises claptrap, and at his rally at Lambert Beach in Brackenridge Park Maverick told the crowd that "every gambler, every communist, and every Nazi in town is supporting the Quin ticket." The election would go into a runoff marred with voter intimidation and irregularities that drew the attention of the Texas Rangers. In the end Quin won.

May 9, 1861

Texas Confederate and Union forces meet in the battle of Adams Hill. The confrontation wasn't actually a battle; no shots were fired. It seemed both sides were eager to avoid bloodshed. The two armies met on Military Road fifteen miles west of San Antonio. Under the terms of the Twiggs surrender of the Department of Texas, federal troops proceeded from Fort Bliss to the Texas coast to join other troops in the evacuation of Texas. After a six-week march from El Paso, the federal army was approached by the rebels, who demanded their unconditional surrender. The Union troops were tired, sick, and outnumbered five to one. They took a defensive position on Adams Hill and, after negotiations, surrendered. They were taken as prisoners of war and held for twenty-one months.

May 10, 1911

Second Lt. George Edward Maurice Kelly is killed during his primary pilot qualification flight at Fort Sam Houston. This was the third aviation accident to happen at Fort Sam in the span of ten days, all of them in a Curtiss

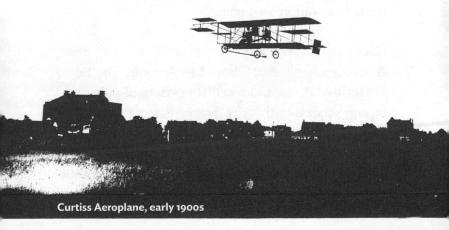

Curtiss Aeroplane, early 1900s

Aeroplane. Kelly was the first American military aviator to be killed while piloting a military aircraft. In 1916 the army created an airfield in San Antonio, initially called Camp Kelly and then Kelly Field. In 1948 it was renamed Kelly Air Force Base.

May 11, 1738

The cornerstone of the San Fernando Cathedral is laid. The cathedral, completed in 1755, was named for King Fernando III of Spain, who was canonized in 1671. While the cathedral has been extensively rebuilt and renovated over the years, the walls of the original structure still form the sanctuary. The church was expanded between 1868 and 1873. The original tower used by Santa Anna during the Battle of the Alamo was torn down. In 1874 San Fernando became an official cathedral when Pope Pius IX named San Antonio a diocese.

May 12, 1946

A polio epidemic shuts down San Antonio. The Board of Health ordered an immediate closing of public and private schools in the city. Brackenridge and all other parks, as well as theaters, dance halls, and other gathering places downtown and north of Commerce Street, were off-limits to anyone under the age of twenty-one. Swimming pools were closed, as were rivers and streams used for swimming. The sale of unpasteurized milk was prohibited. The drastic measures were ordered after eight cases of polio were diagnosed in six days; four were fatal. Mayor Gus B. Mauermann accepted an offer of seventeen planes to spray the city with DDT. A citywide, door-to-door cleanup campaign was announced to address open garbage pits, cesspools, and unsanitary outhouses and privies.

May 13, 1937

A bell stolen from a church in Victoria was recovered from a San Antonio junkyard. The bell was said to have tolled in the Texas seaport of Indianola when the town was destroyed by the 1886 hurricane. The bell weighed more than two hundred pounds, and the junk dealer told police he paid $20 for it. Stamped on the bell was an inscription indicating it was made in Cincinnati in 1871. It was returned to Victoria.

May 14, 1953

Mayor Jack White proposes to the city council that books by Communists in the public library be branded with warning labels. City Manager Wylie Johnson responded that it would be better to "burn the books." The controversy over Communist literature in the library was ignited by Myrtle Glasscock Hance, who compared "un-American activities" listings against the San Antonio Public Library card catalog and found more than five hundred books to object to. She published the list in the pamphlet "REaD READING" and charged twenty-five cents per mimeographed copy. The library board rejected the action. When anti-Communist book forces on the city council became the majority, the library board was replaced with one sympathetic to Hance's views. According to a 1955 article in the *Saturday Review*, "Library director Miss Julia Grothaus and her staff were all intimidated into leaving off purchase lists those books likely to prove objectionable to right-wing trustees." The new board "loaded book and periodical lists with ultra-conservative titles, screened gift books to eliminate those they did not like, and gave favored display to right-wing materials."

May 15, 1861

The *Alamo Express* building on Main Plaza is set on fire. Publisher James P. Newcomb was a rare voice of opposition to the secessionist Knights of the Golden Circle, which used terror tactics to enforce its rule in San Antonio. On May 15 the Golden Circle came to the newspaper's office to lynch Newcomb. Tipped off, he went into hiding. The mob then torched the building. The next day Newcomb was seen on horseback in a full gallop down Commerce Street shouting obscenities at his enemies; he fled to California. In 1867 Newcomb returned to San Antonio and bought an interest in the *San Antonio Express*.

May 16, 1968

Students at Edgewood and Lanier High Schools walk out. It was a year of protests across America against the Vietnam War, poverty, and systemic racial prejudice. In San Antonio the demand for change came with the ten o'clock bell at the underfunded campuses. That was the signal to leave the classroom, grab a protest sign, and march. The list of demands included making improvements to dilapidated facilities, providing access to college prep courses, and lifting the prohibition on speaking Spanish on campus. Soon parents and others joined the cause, pointing out the chronic underfunding of the schools and demanding change.

May 17, 1976

The U.S. Army Arsenal property is offered for sale by the Texas National Guard. The army established the arsenal in 1859 for support in guarding settlements in the frontier. But with the outbreak of the Civil War, Confederate forces claimed the property and ousted the Union troops. When the United States regained control, the complex manufactured cavalry equipment. It was closed in 1948. In 1985 the H. E. Butt Grocery Company bought ten acres of the arsenal complex, rehabilitated existing buildings, and moved its corporate headquarters to San Antonio from Corpus Christi.

May 18, 1987

This is the San Antonio Spurs' lucky day. On this day the struggling basketball team drew the number one pick in the NBA lottery. There was no question who they would draft—David Robinson, a once-in-a-generation franchise player from the Naval Academy. He wouldn't be available to suit up until after his two-year commitment to the navy. Then "the Admiral" played in San Antonio for fourteen seasons. Ten years later to the day, the Spurs won the number one pick again. This time the lottery provided Tim Duncan. David Robinson and Tim Duncan are two of the greatest players to play in the NBA.

May 19, 1992

The San Antonio Water System is created from the consolidation of three agencies: the City Water Board, which was the previous city-owned water utility; the city's wastewater department; and the Alamo Water Conservation and Reuse District. The city council found that the three agencies were not always in agreement when it came to the city's water strategies and voted in December 1991 to establish a single utility responsible for water, wastewater, stormwater, and reuse. The refinancing of $635 million in water and wastewater bonds made the merger possible.

May 20, 1995

The grand opening of the "enchilada red" Central Library is celebrated with a parade of children pulling red wagons filled with books. These were the last books from the old Main Library, at 203 South Saint Mary's Street, which opened in 1968. The Central Library, at 600 Soledad Street, was dramatically different in design and purpose. Ricardo Legorreta, principal architect of the library, designed the building to be inviting, exciting, and impossible to ignore. The passage of a 1989 bond election paid $38 million for the building's construction in Romana Plaza, on the footprint of a Sears store that closed in 1986. No monies, however, were budgeted for books and the newest development in libraries—computers, lots of computers. The San Antonio Public Library Foundation agreed to raise $10 million for the project.

May 21, 1991

Confederate flags and symbols are removed from Robert E. Lee High School. Principal Bill Fish decided to ban the Confederate flag from the school athletic and band uniforms and activities sponsored by the school. The Saint Andrew's Cross flag was not banned from student use. Fish said he made his decision after students said the flag was a symbol of racism. In 2017 the school's name was changed to L.E.E., an acronym for Legacy of

Educational Excellence. The name went into effect in fall 2018.

May 22, 1846 〰〰〰〰〰〰〰〰〰〰〰〰〰〰〰〰〰〰〰〰〰〰〰〰〰〰〰〰〰〰〰〰〰

James L. Trueheart is named San Antonio's first U.S. postmaster. In 1841 Trueheart became the local district court clerk. The entire court was captured a year later when Mexican troops invaded and plundered San Antonio. Trueheart was taken with others to Mexico as a prisoner and incarcerated for two years, returning home in 1844. When he was named postmaster, Texas had just joined the United States. Mail routes had existed during the Republic, but at this time the U.S. post office introduced its first prepaid adhesive stamps, which seemed to announce Texas's new statehood status.

May 23, 1984 〰〰〰〰〰〰〰〰〰〰〰〰〰〰〰〰〰〰〰〰〰〰〰〰〰〰〰〰〰〰〰〰〰

Edgewood v. Kirby is filed. The Mexican American Legal Defense and Educational Fund sued Texas on behalf of Edgewood Independent School District, charging that the state's education funding method, particularly reliance on local property taxes, violated the state constitution. This created inequality in education in property-poor districts like Edgewood. In 1990 the Supreme Court of Texas unanimously declared the system unconstitutional. There have been multiple attempts to fix school funding in the years since, but the problem persists.

May 24, 1911

Mayor Bryan Callaghan Jr. changes the name of Brackenridge Park to Waterworks Park, and the public reacts with outrage. Callaghan and George Brackenridge had long squabbled over water and whiskey. Some had jokingly called the park Prohibition Park over its deed restriction, which stipulated that if alcohol was sold at the park the land would be given to the University of Texas. Callaghan ordered new signs for Waterworks Park, but the public never took to the name, and over a year later the city council changed the name back to Brackenridge Park.

May 25, 2017

San Antonio nurse Genene Jones, dubbed the "angel of death," is charged in the 1981 death of an infant. Jones, who was indicted more than three decades after the child's death, is suspected of killing as many as sixty young children during her time working as a pediatric nurse in San Antonio in the late 1970s to the early 1980s. She had already been convicted of murder and sentenced to ninety-nine years in prison for the 1982 death of fifteen-month-old Chelsea McClellan. She was released from prison due to Texas's mandatory-release regulations and immediately arrested and brought back to Bexar County to face new murder charges. Jones has maintained her innocence. It is suspected that she committed the murders to bring attention to herself as a heroic nurse.

May 26, 1894 〰〰〰〰〰〰〰〰〰〰〰〰〰〰〰〰〰〰〰〰〰〰〰

A crowd gathers outside the Bexar County jail yard on Military Plaza to witness the execution by hanging of Austin Brown, an African American man who was convicted of stalking, ambushing, and murdering a black former police officer, Anderson Harris. It was common for public hangings to occur in San Antonio and across the state. The last Texas execution by hanging was in 1923 in Brazoria County. Texas changed its execution law that year, requiring the death penalty to be carried out by electric chair at the state penitentiary in Huntsville.

May 27, 1988 〰〰〰〰〰〰〰〰〰〰〰〰〰〰〰〰〰〰〰〰〰〰〰

SeaWorld of Texas makes a splash. Its presence was welcomed as an opportunity to boost San Antonio's tourism economy. The 250-acre marine-mammal center and amusement park welcomed seventy-five thousand people on its grand opening and saw 3 million visitors in its first year. The documentary *Blackfish* concerning the controversy of captive killer whales, which were Sea-World's main attraction, was released in 2013. SeaWorld announced in 2016 that it was ending the in-park orca breeding program and would eventually phase out the theatrical killer whale shows. It would now focus on a "Shamu-free future."

May 28, 1857

Outlaw Bill Hart and two of his companions are confronted by Assistant City Marshal Frederick Fieldstrup at the corner of Market and Alamo Streets. After an exchange of words, they pulled their pistols. Fieldstrup killed Hart's companions but was fatally shot. A native of Denmark and a veteran of the U.S.-Mexico War, Fieldstrup is considered the first San Antonio police officer to die in the line of duty since the establishment of a police department. Hart fled but was chased by vigilantes who cornered him. They killed him during the shootout, his body was riddled with bullets.

May 29, 1979

District Judge John H. Wood Jr. is murdered by Charles Harrelson—the first time a federal judge has been killed in connection with duties on the bench. Wood was known as "Maximum John," a nickname he earned for giving drug traffickers maximum prison sentences. Charles Harrelson was allegedly hired for $250,000 by Jamiel "Jimmy" Chagra, a marijuana kingpin operating out of El Paso and Las Vegas who was set to face trial in Wood's courtroom. Chagra was looking at a life sentence without parole. It's reported that he'd initially tried to bribe Wood with $10 million. He was acquitted of the murder-for-hire plot but later confessed to conspiracy in a deal to help his wife, who was also part of the crime. Harrelson was convicted in 1982 and sentenced to two consecutive life terms plus five years. He was found dead in his jail cell in 2007. It's believed the cause was a heart attack.

May 30, 1858

Four men are found hanged from a tree near Mission San José. The four Mexican citizens, Francisco Huizan, Pablo Longoria, Felipe Lopez, and Nicanor Urdiales, were seized by a band of thirty masked men and accused of being horse thieves. But without evidence, documentation, and due process, it's unclear what was truly behind the lynching. The hanging was attributed to the secret "Vigilance Committee." In September 1858 a Bexar County grand jury reported a plague of "summary vengeance" and vigilantism in the community.

May 31, 1874

Temple Beth-El, the oldest Jewish congregation in South Texas, is organized. Temple Beth-El was a charter member of the Union for Reform Judaism. Jewish refugees found their way to Texas and became pioneers, developing a community of merchants, bankers, and cattlemen.

Temple Beth-El, c. 1877

In 1875 the first temple was built at the southeast corner of Travis and Jefferson Streets; its dedication was an interfaith celebration with choirs from the temple and Protestant and Catholic churches singing together. In 1927 Temple Beth-El's current sanctuary, an impressive red-domed structure on Belknap Street and a San Antonio landmark, was constructed.

JUNE

an Antonians of a certain age probably remember the *Captain Gus Show*, an afternoon children's program on KENS-TV featuring cartoons. The captain, Joe Alston, donned an orange wig, a yachting hat, and an exaggerated handlebar mustache. It was a typical television kiddie show of the era replete with corny jokes and silly skits. The captain had a small audience area of bleachers on the soundstage where he could meet his "mateys" and ask their name and age, questions that seemed like life-or-death queries to the nervous kids peering into the face of their television idol holding the *Matey Manual*. This book must have appeared a voluminous tome with the rules of comportment for a life filled with values—values like the ones exemplified by cartoon hero Popeye against the dastardly Bluto, he of the small head, no neck, considerable girth, and loose and lusty morals.

Not even a train barreling toward Popeye as he was tied to the tracks could stop him. He'd suck that can of spinach down through his pipe, *y santo remedio*: His arms would unfurl into magnificent biceps. The ropes and chains that held him fell away like water. With one eye closed, he punched Bluto and sent him into the stratosphere. He even punched the anthropomorphic train in the nose and stopped it dead in its tracks.

Only one thing could stop Popeye, and that was Watergate. The hearings were televised starting in 1972, pre-empting *Captain Gus* and most other television shows.

One had only to change the channel to the Spanish-language television station. Our *madrecitas* and *abuelas* were happy with the programming change, as the onomatopoeic sounds of cartoons were replaced by the patter and murmurs of star-crossed lovers or the resolute monologue of a sneering villain on a telenovela.

On May 1, 1946, the FCC granted a broadcasting license to Raoul Cortez for KCOR-AM 1350. Cortez wanted to broadcast Spanish-language news, but he had to wait due to a ban on non-English-language broadcasting during World War II. On June 10, 1955, Cortez's sister station, KCOR-TV 41, signed on the airwaves as the nation's first Spanish-language television station.

Cortez's son-in-law, Emilio Nicolas Sr., went on to make the TV station a financial success and built a second station in Los Angeles. This formed the foundation of the first Spanish-language television network in the country: Univision.

In the 1840s the Native American Party, also known as the American Party or the Know-Nothings, was opposed to Irish and German Catholic immigrants. They believed in the principle of nationality, which they stood behind to justify warnings against Native peoples and, in 1846, against Mexico.

Many protested the war with Mexico, including Abraham Lincoln and Henry David Thoreau. The latter went to jail rather than pay taxes to contribute to the war. President Polk's stance was to push the Mexican army out of Texas, take New Mexico and California, and march on to Mexico City. The war's official end came in February 1848 with the signing of the Treaty of Guadalupe Hidalgo.

Before the treaty signing, San Antonio was under Mexican rule. The Mexican Americans in this part of the country are twice conquered, first by Spain in the 1600s and then by the United States in 1848. But the echoes of the Spanish language have never quite been silenced. That's rather difficult to believe given the number of viral videos, even today, that expose the disdain and hatred some have for the language or those who speak it. Generations of San Antonians remember schoolhouse wrist slaps or other punitive measures dealt to those who dared speak Spanish.

Today one can drive along our complicated highway system and see billboards in Spanish, but the conflict is not resolved. Sure, Pepto Bismol can appropriate the *sana, sana colita de rana* singsong curative incantation of many a Mexican American childhood as its slogan. Its bubble-gum pink antidote belies the bitter reality of our history, however, and the inherent injustices that have gone with it for centuries. And that's not kid stuff.

June 1, 1929

The Tower Life Building, which rises 403 feet and has thirty floors, is completed. Originally dubbed the Smith-Young Tower, the eight-sided, neo-Gothic brick and terra-cotta tower (complete with gargoyles) has helped define San Antonio's skyline for decades. In the 1940s the building was renamed the Transit Tower for the San Antonio Transit Company, which Smith Brothers purchased. The building is now named for its current owner, Tower Life Insurance. In 1991 it was added to the National Register of Historic Places

June 2, 1931

Texas governor Ross Sterling signs the San Antonio River Canal and Conservancy Bill, seen as the first major step in the grand plan to make the river navigable to 150 miles from the Gulf of Mexico. The bill also created a district in Bexar County that would allow bond issues for water improvements and levy taxes to maintain the district. The plan called for using locks and dams to make the river navigable for large barges for cargo shipping. This was a persistent vision for the city's development until the 1970s, and while it was never achieved, the bill created

Tower Life Building, 2014

the taxing district that would eventually become the San Antonio River Authority.

June 3, 1899

The cornerstone is laid and dedicated for a Confederate monument in Travis Park. Judge John Henninger Reagan, who served in the Confederate States of America as postmaster general in the cabinet of Jefferson Davis, was the guest orator for the ceremony. According to the *Light* newspaper, Reagan was greeted with cheers as he stood to give his remarks, "in which he reviewed the causes of the Civil War and its progress. Naturally, he took a Confederate view of it but he was moderate and political in his views." The monument was removed from the park in September 2017 after public opinion turned against honoring the Confederacy.

June 4, 1917

San Antonio must shut down its brothels. City leaders agreed to the demands of the secretary of the army, who was concerned that the high rate of venereal disease in troops stationed in San Antonio was affecting their combat readiness. The city was told to shut down the "sporting district" or the army would move its divisional training camps elsewhere. Mayor Sam C. Bell immediately ordered the police to close the red-light district west of San Pedro Creek. Six months later the joint city-military committee found that prostitution was still raging and declared that "the Police Department was derelict in its duty."

June 5, 1969

The University of Texas at San Antonio is established. At the time San Antonio was the only major American city without a public university. In a ceremony in front of the Alamo, Governor Preston Smith signed the law creating the university, quite literally on the back of state representative Frank Lombardino, who Smith said carried the bill on his broad back through the legislature. UTSA's first administrative offices were set up in 1970 at HemisFair Park. Classes began at the Loop 1604 campus in 1975.

June 6, 1836

One hundred eighteen years of presidio presence in San Antonio comes to a close. After the Texas Revolution, Capt. Francisco de Castañeda withdrew from San Antonio and turned the city over to Capt. Juan Seguín, commander of Republic of Texas forces in San Antonio. As Castañeda led his small detachment out of Béxar, he left behind the presidio's extensive historic archive and records. Perhaps he thought his absence would be temporary, but in abandoning the presidio's historic library he gave San Antonio ownership of its documents and its story.

June 7, 1968

Students protest Bexar County commissioner A. J. Ploch for comments he made in the CBS documentary *Hunger in America*, which showed the disturbing poverty of Mexican Americans living on San Antonio's West Side. In the CBS interview the longtime politician said there was no poverty in San Antonio and that the people who were poor refused to work and "ain't worth a dime." The documentary was controversial in San Antonio, and the local CBS affiliate refused to air it during primetime, scheduling it for 11 p.m.

June 8, 1937

Pompeo Coppini is named sculptor for the monument to the heroes of the Alamo. The controversial $100,000 contract was awarded over the objections of celebrated Texas author and historian J. Frank Dobie, who was on the historical advisory board for the cenotaph commission. Dobie called the deal with Coppini a betrayal of the Alamo, and said the Alamo didn't need a monument because the Alamo was its own monument. He complained that politics had tainted the process for creating a public space for future generations to honor the heroes of the Alamo. The cenotaph was built on Alamo Plaza and dedicated on November 11, 1940.

June 9, 1926

Mayor John Tobin announces his plans to beautify the San Antonio River. He called to convert the unimproved river that wound through the business district into a veritable fairyland that would rival the beauty of the canals of Venice. Tobin ordered the riverbanks' stone walls to be festooned with multicolored lights and called for the removal of unsightly overhanging walls and shacks. He also wanted electric ornamental fountains spaced in the middle of the river so they could be viewed from the street bridges. "The river is one of San Antonio's real assets," Tobin said. "And we are to develop plans that will make it a thing of real beauty and something visitors will remember and comment on long after they leave the city."

June 10, 1955

With three days of live performances by many of the biggest international stars of Spanish-language entertainment, KCOR-TV 41 signs on the airwaves as the nation's first Spanish-language television station. The call letters were taken from sister station KCOR-AM, named for owner Raoul Cortez and the country's first full-time Spanish-language radio station. On May 1, 1946, the FCC granted a broadcasting license to KCOR-AM 1350. Cortez, who was a journalist, civil rights leader, and entrepreneur, applied for the license in 1944, but non-English broadcasting was banned during World War II. He argued that Spanish-language news would bolster Mexican American support for the war but nevertheless had to wait for the war's end to sign on. In 1961 KCOR-TV was sold to his son-in-law Emilio Nicolas Sr. and became KUAL-TV. Nicolas was able to make the station a financial success and built a second station, KMEX-TV, in Los Angeles. This formed the foundation of the country's first Spanish-language television network, which came to be Univision. The San Antonio station changed its call sign again to KWEX-TV.

June 11, 1955

The first African American student enrolls at San Antonio College and is greeted by stunned silence. W. P. Mccurly, dean of the school, refused to comment, saying he would wait for the college board's decision on the matter. Hubert F. Lindsey, the barrier-breaking student, was seeking to enroll in premed night classes not available at Saint Philip's College, the local historic black college. School officials said Lindsey was carefully screened and met all the criteria for admission. San Antonio College president James Loftin predicted that soon all segregation barriers would be removed.

June 12, 1990

With concerns about the content of 2 Live Crew's album *As Nasty as They Wanna Be*, the San Antonio police department orders area record stores to stop selling what they call "indecent" material. All but Dave Risher of Hogwild Records complied. On June 20 Risher was arrested on the charge of distributing obscene material after he sold a cassette of the rap album to a twenty-year-old who was part of a local anti-pornography crusade. Risher refused to plead guilty and fought the charge on constitutional grounds. Six months later, just as the case was heading to court, the charge was suddenly dropped.

June 13, 1945

An Alamo City Salute to War Victors in downtown San Antonio is turned into a celebration for war heroes from Europe. VE Day, when Allies accepted Germany's surrender, was May 8, but the war in the Pacific still loomed. That victory would come in September. Meanwhile San Antonio held a ticker tape parade for the returning warriors. The route went in front of the Alamo, where a corral of cattle was set up for the occasion. In one of the parade cars was a smiling freckle-faced soldier from Farmersville, Texas: Lt. Audie Murphy, recipient of the Medal of Honor.

June 14, 1937

Charles Bellinger dies. A successful businessman, gambler, and political force, Bellinger was known as the "Black Boss" of San Antonio. He paid poll taxes for thousands of African American voters, and they followed his recommendations at the ballot box. This gave Bellinger the power to swing local elections for a price that included paving streets in front of African American churches and improvements for black education. Bellinger pleaded guilty to tax evasion and was sentenced to eighteen months. President Franklin Delano Roosevelt commuted his sentence after local leaders petitioned for a pardon. Critics say his prosecution was politically motivated.

June 15, 1903

San Antonio gets a library. Steel baron and billionaire Andrew Carnegie gave the city $50,000 for a library if the city would provide the site and budget $5,000 a year for maintenance. The Kampmann family donated the land at the corner of Market and Presa Streets. The grand building was badly damaged in the 1921 flood, and in 1930 the library was rebuilt in an art deco style. In 1968 it became the home of the Hertzberg Circus Museum, which is now the site of the Briscoe Western Art Museum.

June 16, 1936

The municipal airport's name is changed from Winburn Field back to Stinson Field. The city first changed the airport's name on October 31, 1927, in honor of William D. Winburn, a reporter for the *San Antonio Light* who died in a plane crash along with four others. A petition signed

Katherine Stinson, c. 1910

by members of the San Antonio Aeronautical Association and airmen working at the field requested that the city restore the airport's original name. The petitioners argued that the Stinson family did more for San Antonio's legacy of aviation than any other. They operated the Stinson School of Flying, one of the first in the nation to train World War I pilots. Marjorie Stinson was the world's youngest woman pilot, and Jack Stinson was the world's youngest "boy pilot." Eddie Stinson, world famous for his air exploits, discovered how to conquer the dreaded tail-spin. Katherine Stinson, who was trained by the Wright Brothers, was the fourth woman to receive a pilot's license. Known as the "flying schoolgirl," she traveled the world putting on flying exhibitions and performing such feats as diving a thousand feet, racing automobiles, and turning loops. She was the first skywriter and the first woman to perform the loop the loop.

June 17, 1971

The Texas governor signs S.B. 513, also known as the "Clean Up Mitchell Lake Bill," into law. For years residents in South San Antonio complained of a foul odor coming from the lake in south Bexar County, which was being used by the city to dump sewage. The legislation prohibited the city from continuing the practice. The city opposed the bill, complaining it would be forced to spend millions on upgrading its sewage plant. The San Antonio Water System has taken over management of Mitchell Lake and teamed up with the National Audubon Society develop the 1,200-acre site as a natural resource, a favorite of bird watchers.

June 18, 1856

A caravan of camels parades through San Antonio. Secretary of War Jefferson Davis hoped the legendary "ships of the desert" would be the answer to securing

West Texas. Seventy-five camels were imported from the Syria region to Indianola, Texas, and moved inland. Major Henry C. Wayne of the U.S. Quartermaster's Department, who commanded the camel operations, wrote in his journal that he "moved slowly, both on account of their recent sea-trip, and for the little ones that were unable to march long." Wayne arranged with San Antonio to temporarily station the camel corps at San Pedro Springs. To get there the camels made an impromptu parade down Main Street. Later they operated out of Camp Verde and Fort Davis. In 1860 the camels were ordered by Col. Robert E. Lee to march to Big Bend. The results of the ambitious experiment were mixed. The camels outperformed horses and mules, but several died on the trek. Many of the soldiers developed a fondness for the creatures, but others suffered from camel culture clash, claiming they smelled bad, had a terrible temperament, and frightened the horses and mules. It's likely that the Civil War doomed the camel experiment.

June 19, 1954

A fiery cross is discovered in front of Woodlawn Pool at Woodlawn Lake Park. The trademark symbol of the Ku Klux Klan was ignited at the public pool the day after six African American youth defied Jim Crow and went swimming. As a result, city leaders discovered there was no segregation ordinance on the city books and ordered all city pools closed for "maintenance and repairs." The city council called an emergency meeting and voted to ban people of color from city pools. After a lawsuit was filed, the ordinance was repealed two years later.

June 20, 1922

An insurance company is born. Twenty-five army officers were unable to purchase auto insurance because of the perception that they were a high-risk group. Their solution was to form a pool to insure each other's vehicles. Maj. Walter Moore had the first policy for his 1922 Elcar and became the first member of the United States Army Automobile Association. In 1924 the name was changed to United States Automobile Association, or USAA. The organization began offering home and life insurance in the 1960s and banking insurance in the 1980s. USAA employs more than thirty-two thousand people worldwide.

June 21, 1882

Oscar Wilde, the Irish poet and playwright, gives a lecture at Turner Opera House at the corner of Saint Mary's and Houston Streets. Admission was one dollar. At twenty-seven years of age, Wilde had yet to write noted works like *The Picture of Dorian Gray*, but he was already famous for being famous. The newspaper account paid special attention to Wilde's appearance, which included shoulder-length hair, a black velvet suit, silk stockings, and a large white ribbon around his neck. In 1895 Wilde was put on trial for "gross indecency"—essentially for homosexuality. He would serve two years in prison and die soon after, at the age of forty-six.

June 22, 1857

James E. Birch is awarded the contract for a southern mail route. Designated Route 8076, the first contract for overland service on the route provided for a semi-monthly service in four-horse coaches scheduled to leave San Antonio and San Diego on the ninth and the twenty-fourth of each month, with thirty days allowed for each trip. On July 9 a mail train left San Antonio. Pack animals carried the mailbags, leading to the nickname the "Jackass Express." The first journey took fifty-three days, a new record for overland mail.

June 23, 2005

Ramiro "Ram" Ayala, owner of the bar Taco Land, is murdered in a robbery that netted the assailants $200. Before the Pearl development made the near downtown area an attractive destination for hipsters, Taco Land, on West Grayson Street, was selling beer in a can for cheap. With his profanity-punctuated vocabulary, seventy-two-year-old Ayala welcomed bikers, blue-collar workers, and underground rockers. It looked dark and dangerous, but the bar provided a space for any local punk band that just wanted to play. It became a haven for those in the music scene and eventually attracted touring bands. The resulting mashup of the working-class ethos with punk culture created a panorama that was *puro* San Antonio. Along with Ayala, doorman Douglas Morgan was killed. Jose Najera pleaded guilty to the robbery and was sentenced to fifty years in prison. His accomplice, Joseph Gamboa, was convicted in 2007 and is on Texas death row.

June 24, 1970

A Bexar County special grand jury report depicts an "abysmal picture of the narcotics menace" in the San Antonio area. The report stated that the illegal drug problem "poses a great threat to our citizens from a criminal point of view." The authors claimed there were an estimated three thousand known addicts in Bexar County with a drug habit requiring $50 a day. "The only source of money is obviously through crime," the report stated. The jurors recommended continuous narcotics education in the schools and through the media, churches, and homes.

June 25, 1999

The San Antonio Spurs win their first NBA championship. Because of a labor disagreement between players and owners, 1999 saw a shortened season. The Spurs had a six-to-eight start but went on to win thirty-one of their remaining thirty-six games and have the league's best record. When it came to the finals there was no shortage of intensity. With forty-seven seconds to go in the fifth game of the series, Avery Johnson hit the game winner and the Spurs beat the New York Knicks to clinch the championship. Tim Duncan was named the series MVP. The Spurs went on to win five NBA championship rings.

June 26, 1917

Thirty-three veterans of the Spanish-American War join together to form a Veterans of Foreign Wars Post, the first in the state. During its first three decades, VFW Post 76 was without a permanent home, and members met in a variety of locations, including the Spanish Governor's Palace and area churches. In 1946 the post leased and then bought a Queen Anne–style home, built in 1895, for $15,000. The two-story white building, with its impressive columns and wraparound veranda, backs onto the San Antonio River's museum reach. The VFW house is open to the public.

June 27, 1884

The last members of the notorious Helotes Gang are captured near San Angelo. Desperados Lewis Potter and James McDaniel were known as "holy terrors" along the San Angelo–Abilene trail, where they would prey on stagecoaches and mail delivery. The two were transferred to Bexar County, tried for murder, and sentenced to life in prison. But before he could be sent to prison, McDaniel escaped and fled to the Hill Country. He was tracked to a goat camp near Boerne and refused to surrender. In the resulting gun battle, the outlaw was killed.

June 28, 1929

Following a series of disastrous floods, including one in 1921 that killed more than fifty people, the city looks for a plan for the downtown portion of the San Antonio River. Architect Robert H. H. Hugman presented his vision, which he called the "Shops of Romula and Aragon," to Mayor C. M. Chambers, city commissioners, and down town property owners. The proposal called for upgrades to the river's downtown bypass to control flooding but also maintained the river's natural beauty. Although not as extensive as his original proposal, the controversial project resulted in improvement of more than twenty-one blocks known today as the River Walk.

June 29, 1956

Rock and roll records are removed from juke boxes at city swimming pools because of "undesirable incidents" that, according to the assistant director of parks, were caused by the music. Complaints focused on wild dancing in swimming suits and "rougher elements loafing around

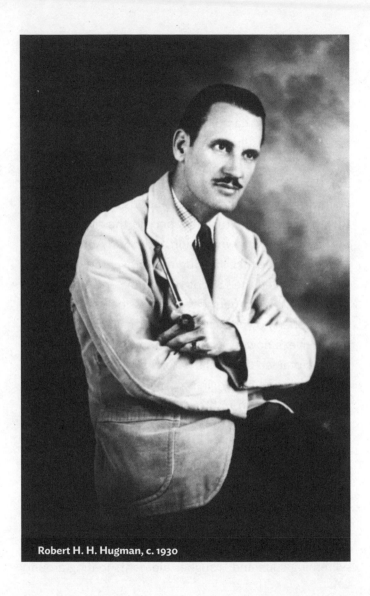

Robert H. H. Hugman, c. 1930

and causing trouble." The records were replaced by singles that officials said "were not designed to set one's feet on fire."

June 30, 1937 \\\

Vigorous protests are sent to Mayor C. K. Quin by members of the Workers Alliance of America the day after San Antonio police officers smashed their headquarters and arrested several members, including their leader, twenty-year-old Emma Tenayuca. Quin said he regretted the destruction but refused to take action. Sixteen policemen had raided the headquarters at 905 West Travis Street and smashed the furniture, a piano, and a typewriter into pieces. The conflict began when the alliance began a protest at the Works Progress Administration offices in the Gunter Hotel over their cutting of work relief jobs from the area. Tenayuca and others were charged with unlawful assembly and disturbing the peace. Police chief Owen Kilday claimed literature in the headquarters was "communistic" and said, "That just backs up my contention that the Tenayuca woman is nothing but a paid agitator sent here to stir up trouble among the ignorant Mexicans." Despite a writ of habeas corpus, Judge W. W. McCrory refused to release Tenayuca, saying, "She belongs in jail. Let her stay there!" He said she was nothing but "a damned communist" and he didn't care what the police did with her.

JULY

arry Hertzberg was an attorney and state senator in 1919 and again in 1921. He and his business associate, Tom Scaperlanda, donated the country's oldest public circus collection to the San Antonio Public Library, and it is now in the Witte Museum. Hertzberg is also known for having donated fifteen thousand rare books to the library.

In 1942 the *New Yorker*'s Mark Murphy reported that the Ringling Brothers and Barnum & Bailey Sideshow was experiencing a "blight" due to the war. Fred Smythe, the show's manager, claimed that the war and improved sanitary conditions in the country meant there were fewer and fewer "weird" people he could hire. He admitted that he regularly received mail from people proclaiming they were "freaks." They were, he said, "people who think they are sufficiently odd to be exhibited," but often the talents they claimed to have never materialized beyond, for instance, a woman saying she would allow her whiskers to grow in order to be touted as a bearded lady.

Barbette, whose given name was Vander Clyde Broadway, grew up in Round Rock, Texas, at the turn of the century. When he was young his mother took him to the circus, and he was engrossed by the high-wire act. He worked picking cotton to make money to go see the act as often as possible. It's been widely reported that he practiced for hours by walking along his mother's steel clothesline. Eager to strike out on his own, he graduated from high school at age fourteen, beginning his career in earnest after he answered an ad to join the Alfaretta Sisters aerialist team. One of the sisters had died, and Barbette auditioned in San Antonio to take her place in the act.

Barbette and the remaining sister noticed that the act seemed much more dramatic and death-defying when performed by women. Something about the incongruity of the women's clothes (full petticoat ensembles in that era) made the act more impressive. The sister asked Barbette if he'd be willing to dress as a girl; he agreed. He traveled the world, including to England and Paris, where he appeared at the Moulin Rouge and the Folies Bergère. He later became a featured attraction with Ringling Brothers and Barnum & Bailey Circus.

The end of Barbette's long career, one championed by French poet and artist Jean Cocteau (with whom he had an affair), came in the early 1940s when the effects of a fall, pneumonia, polio, and poor health rendered him immobile. After rehabilitation, he became an artistic director and aerialist trainer, eventually returning to Texas, where he lived in Austin with his sister and later committed suicide.

Before Barbette's heyday, vaudeville stars and conjoined twins Daisy and Violet Hilton won their independence from their managers Edith and Meyer Meyers.

England natives, the girls lived in a San Antonio mansion when not touring. In 1931 the sisters sued the Meyerses for their independence in Bexar County, gaining freedom from their contract and $100,000 in damages.

In the *New Yorker* interview Smythe said, "Things are always happening to freaks and to people who have got to make a living through their peculiarities.... You know we even call freaks strange people. More polite. They like to call themselves 'performers,' although God knows all the performing they do is standing up or sitting down."

In 2013, another court case involved a strip club dispute with the City of San Antonio over how much clothing exotic dancers should wear. In a pun-filled and double entendre–laden decision denying a preliminary injunction to the strip club, U.S. district judge Fred Biery of San Antonio referenced a contortionist, Velma Adkerson, who had performed fully clothed as Miss Wiggles in the city in the '60s.

Adkerson's obituary in the October 12, 2012, edition of the *Anchorage Daily News* asserts that "owners of all-white clubs during the era of segregation used her as a so-called 'break-in' act, a comic yet appreciable exotic diversion that their audiences would accept in an otherwise all-white lineup—subtly opening the door to other black performers." She had enjoyed a long run at the Eastwood Club in San Antonio and had been dancing at

Jack Ruby's club in Dallas when President John F. Kennedy was assassinated.

Like Barbette, Adkerson had suffered the merciless effects of polio. Because charities helped her when she was hospitalized and could not work, she spent her life paying it forward. Mourners at her funeral attested to her magnanimity. It is reported that for years she made clothes for friends and the children of her community. She created runway fashion shows featuring a diversity of models, some of whom wore size twenty, and ranging in age from fifteen to seventy.

Though many knew Adkerson as Miss Wiggles, she once noted that "people don't know me for who I am."

July 1, 1941

"Scrap to scrap the Axis." That was a slogan on the lips of San Antonians as they joined a local drive for aluminum for national defense. The attack on Pearl Harbor wouldn't happen for another five months, but it was clear that America's involvement with the war in Europe was imminent. San Antonio police officers took the lead in the collection campaign and rounded up scrap metal. Twenty-six Lone Star Brewery drivers volunteered on their days off to collect the metal. Families were encouraged to drop off their old pots, pans, and other articles in front of Municipal Auditorium.

July 2, 1731

The San Fernando church site is selected when Juan Antonio Pérez de Almazán, captain of the Béxar presidio, lays out a central square for the villa of San Fernando de Béxar. He followed instructions by the Spanish government for the newly arrived Canary Islanders. The church, located on the square's west side, was completed in 1755. The congregation chose Our Lady of Candelaria and Nuestra Señora de Guadalupe as patrons in addition to the town's patron, San Fernando, or King Fernando III of Spain.

July 3, 1963

A location is announced for HemisFair, at the southeast corner of downtown. The 150-acre site for the proposed 1968 World's Fair would supplant one of the city's oldest neighborhoods, known as Germantown, which had once been farmland for the Alamo mission. In 1963 San Antonio leaders saw Germantown as a slum, and Mayor Walter McAllister called for immediate "horseback appraisals of the land" to start the process of condemning and acquisition. HemisFair opened less than five years later.

July 4, 1976

The remains of Juan Seguín return to Texas. Seguín was a hero of the Texas Revolution, a senator in the Republic, and mayor of San Antonio. A member of a prominent

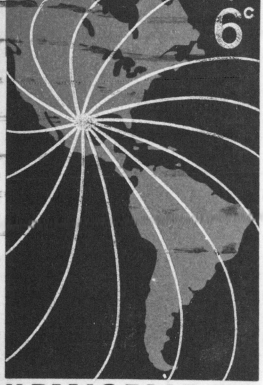

HemisFair commemorative stamp

South Texas ranching family, he fought for the rights of Tejanos. While he was mayor, Anglo squatters accused him of being a traitor to Texas. He fled to Mexico, where he was imprisoned until he agreed to serve in the Mexican military. He died there in 1890. Eighty-six years later his remains were buried in Seguín, the town named in his honor.

July 5, 2015

The San Antonio Missions National Historical Park is named a UN World Heritage Site. It was the first time the United Nations Educational, Scientific and Cultural Organization deemed a Texas site of "outstanding cultural or natural importance to the common heritage of humanity." The decision capped a nine-year campaign by the city to have the early eighteenth-century missions listed alongside the Statue of Liberty, Yellowstone, the Grand Canyon, and other key cultural landmarks.

July 6, 1951

Documents filed with the state comptroller reveal that Marion Koogler McNay has bequeathed her estate to art. When McNay, a prominent San Antonio philanthropist, died on April 12, 1950, her estate was valued at approximately $1.5 million. Of that sum about $1 million was earmarked for an art institute. It was directed that the art museum and school be set up on the grounds of McNay's twenty-three-acre estate on North New Braunfels Avenue. The total value of her personal art collection was $331,445 in 1951 dollars. It included thirty modern French oil paintings, twenty-nine modern French watercolors, eighteen American oil paintings, and twelve modern French and American drawings. McNay also held bonds in many local public works, including the Spanish Governor's Palace and city parks, bridges, and the library. The McNay Art Museum, the first modern art museum in the state, opened its doors to the public on November 3, 1954, with an exhibition of works by Pablo Picasso.

July 7, 1939

San Antonio congressman Maury Maverick campaigns for reelection on the city's West Side. The area was known as a stronghold of the vote-harvesting machine that had kept Maverick's political enemies in power. About three thousand spectators attended the rally, which started with the showing of a humorous cartoon and a performance by a hillbilly band before Maverick took the stage. Standing in front of a large American flag, speaking English and Spanish, he touted his pork-barrel success in Washington and his liberal credentials: "Any man who wants to parade the streets with a sign has the right to do so. And no rich man should have the right to buy a chief of police and have him knock people in the head and throw them in jail." He also said: "Who was it hit you over the head? Chief of police Owen Kilday. Who was it put you in jail? Kilday and Mayor Quin." Maverick was being challenged for the congressional seat by Paul Kilday, brother of the police chief. Amid election day shenanigans Kilday won and remained in Congress until 1961.

July 8, 1931

Outrage from the white community living near the proposed site of a "negro school" forces the San Antonio school board to abandon plans to build a school at Palmetto and Nebraska Streets. Residents complained that the school would be across the street from Pittman-Sullivan Park, and the presence of the black students would interfere with park activities. The park was a dividing line between the city's black and white communities. In the past, "various occurrences" between white and black children in the park had caused authorities to bar "negroes" from the park. The school board found a new location for the school at Burleson and Gevers Streets. Phillis Wheatley High School was dedicated on December 20, 1933, and remained open through the 1969–70 school year. The San Antonio Independent School District integrated in 1955.

July 9, 1912

One of the largest funerals in city history is held for Bryan "King" Callaghan Jr., who was mayor for nine terms—eighteen years total, not all of them consecutive. He also served two terms as county judge. His Irish immigrant father, Bryan Callaghan Sr., was mayor from 1847 to 1849, and his son Alfred Callaghan would serve as mayor from 1947 to 1949. Callaghan Jr. died from a long illness, while in office. He laid the foundation for a political machine that would survive after his death, with election rigging, cronyism, job patronage, and a tolerance of gambling and brothels. But Callaghan had a reputation of not being personally corrupt to enrich himself.

July 10, 2015

After 110 years at the Alamo, the Daughters of the Republic of Texas mark the end of their custodianship. As tourists continued their casual inspection of the Shrine to Texas Liberty, there was a solemn ceremony. In an emotional service, the Daughters recited prayers—in English, Spanish, Danish, and German—to remember the fallen Alamo defenders. The Daughters turned over authority of the hallowed grounds to the Texas General Land Office. Tears were shed as bagpipes played "The Yellow Rose of Texas."

July 11, 1882

Jack Harris is fatally gunned down. In 1872 Harris, a San Antonio businessman and political leader, opened the Vaudeville Theater and Saloon at the corner of

Commerce Street on Main Plaza. A magnet for outlaws, it was the most notorious place in Texas for drinking, gambling, and other vices. In 1880 gunslinger and Austin marshal Ben Thompson lost heavily at the tables and threatened revenge. Thompson returned two years later. After an exchange of profane threats and insults through the Vaudeville's swinging door, Thompson was quicker on the draw with his six-shooter than Harris with his shotgun and fired the fatal shots into the saloon. Harris's obituaries saluted "his liberality, shrewdness, and tact."

July 12, 1936

San Antonio mayor C. K. Quin fires the entire Board of Health. The board was charged with finding ways to reduce the local tuberculosis death rate and to deal with outbreaks of polio and other infectious diseases. Their recommendation was to consolidate the city, county, and school health departments and to give the health board authority to hire and fire health employees. Doctors who made up the board said Quin's actions were unethical. He would later be indicted for using the health department's payroll to fund his political machine. He was also accused of using the office and employees of the health department as a front to run his criminal activities, including gambling, prostitution, and selling bootleg liquor.

July 13, 1955

The San Antonio Independent School District announces that segregation is over and that integration of African American and white students will begin in fall 1955 at the district's ninety schools. The school board unanimously passed a resolution directing Superintendent Thomas Portwood to prepare for integration "at the earliest possible date." The U.S. Supreme Court had issued its landmark decision *Brown v. Board of Education* a year earlier, on May 17, 1954. The court found that state laws establishing racial segregation in public schools were unconstitutional and that "separate educational facilities are inherently unequal." There was no dissension and little discussion before the vote, which the board admitted was "historic." This was the first local school district to take up the question and end segregation.

July 14, 1955

"How Kelly Field Spends Your Tax Dollars" is published by sheet-metal worker Roy Harrington. The fifteen-page booklet cost twenty-five cents but could have cost Kelly Air Force Base much more as it detailed idleness and waste. Harrington said workers often stood around with nothing to do for days at a time. He said he wanted the facility to be more thrifty and efficient, so he sent copies of his work to President Eisenhower and Senator Lyndon Johnson. Johnson nixed an investigation into the allegations. Kelly officials said the pamphlet was untrue, misleading, and ridiculous.

July 15, 1947 〰〰〰〰〰〰〰〰〰〰〰〰〰〰〰〰〰〰〰〰〰〰〰〰

The San Antonio branch office of the Sugar Rationing Administration is closed. But there was no sugarcoating the fact that sixteen employees were given pink slips. After the attack on Pearl Harbor and America's entrance into World War II, restrictions on food and other materials were necessary for the war effort. On January 30, 1942, the Emergency Price Control Act granted the Office of Price Administration authority to set prices and ration food and commodities. By the spring Americans were unable to purchase sugar without government-issued food coupons. To administer the program, offices were established across the nation. The San Antonio office was in the Transit Tower.

July 16, 1934 〰〰〰〰〰〰〰〰〰〰〰〰〰〰〰〰〰〰〰〰〰〰〰〰〰〰〰〰

The pecan shellers go on strike. The Pecan Shelling Workers Union of San Antonio was formed in 1933 by Magdaleno Rodriguez. There were competing organizers of *los nueceros*, the pecan shellers. Julius Seligmann, the city's major shelling operator, was paying Rodriguez to weaken rival shellers. Rodriguez did win some concessions for the workers. Later he was jailed for union activities and confined to a mental hospital. Four years later Emma Tenayuca managed to unite San Antonio's fractured labor movement and led the first successful pecan sheller strike.

A pecan sheller, 1939

July 17, 1924 〰〰〰〰〰〰〰〰〰〰〰〰〰〰〰〰〰〰〰〰〰〰〰

San Antonio is the largest city in Texas. The U.S. Census Bureau pegged San Antonio's population at 191,398. Dallas was the second-largest city in the state at the time, at just over 189,000. Mayor John W. Tobin predicted that by 1950 the city would hit 600,000. Through most of San Antonio's history it was the largest city in the state, but its population growth stalled in the 1930s during the Depression. Dallas and Houston meanwhile saw rapid growth due to the oil boom. San Antonio's population wouldn't hit the 600,000 mark until the 1960s.

July 18, 1970 〰〰〰〰〰〰〰〰〰〰〰〰〰〰〰〰〰〰〰〰〰〰〰

The Brackenridge Eagle is stopped by two gunmen after pulling out of the park's tunnel. Many of the seventy-five passengers on the miniature train thought the holdup was part of a show and laughed when the pistoleros demanded their valuables. When the marauders started to get rough, passengers realized they were part of the first train robbery in Texas in the last fifty years. The thieves got away with about $5,000. After a manhunt they were found to be soldiers stationed at Fort Sam Houston.

July 19, 1949 〰〰〰〰〰〰〰〰〰〰〰〰〰〰〰〰〰〰〰〰〰〰〰

The first leg of the interregional highway is opened to traffic. The section of highway, which ran from the intersection of Woodlawn Avenue and Fredericksburg

Road to Culebra Road, was San Antonio's introduction to smooth highway driving, but locals were slow to adopt the new commute. Just six months later, on December 8, voters turned out for special election for a $4 million bond issue pegged for more highway construction. It passed three to one. More highway miles were built, and the interregional highway became part of I-10.

July 20, 1956

As the Civil Rights Act is debated in Washington, D.C., two burning crosses are discovered in San Antonio. Police reported the burning of a six-foot cross wrapped in burlap and soaked in gasoline. The cross was found in the evening, shortly before ten o'clock, near the corner of Hildebrand and McCullough Avenues. This was the city's second cross burning in a week. The first one was at Highway 90 and Commerce Street. The Civil Rights Act of 1957 was the first federal civil rights legislation passed since 1875.

July 21, 1865

Songbooks and wine are passed out at the Alamo to celebrate raising the Union flag over the Alamo to mark the end of the Civil War. The war had ended four months earlier, but the news had just reached the frontier. Leading the celebration was Wilhelm Carl August Thielepape, a German-born engineer, architect, lithographer, and composer who came to San Antonio in 1854 and helped to organize the city's German-English School. As a Union sympathizer, he likely spent the war in Eagle Pass or Mexico. He was appointed mayor of San Antonio during Reconstruction, beginning November 8, 1867. He spent much of his time working to bring a rail line to the city, settling the school system, and restoring the city's relationship with the U.S. military. The U.S. Army was considering establishing its headquarters in other parts of Texas, but on February 23, 1868, Thielepape negotiated a deal with the army to remain in San Antonio. Thielepape promised to provide the army some city property in an area that would eventually become Fort Sam Houston.

July 22, 1932

The White Primary system is challenged. A federal district court in San Antonio grants African American C. A. Booker an injunction to force Democratic Party officials to allow him to vote in the July 23 primary. Nonwhites were prohibited from voting in Texas Democratic primaries, which during this single-party era essentially elected all of the state's public officials. Maury Maverick, a prominent liberal who had claimed he would fight to protect the constitutional rights of black Americans, leapt into action to have the injunction overturned and keep the White Primary system in place. He was eventually successful, but not before more than a thousand black Texans voted in the primary. Maverick's support for the system was rooted in his opposition to the city's corrupt machine politics and the selling of black votes by Charles Bellinger. The White Primary was eventually ruled unconstitutional by the U.S. Supreme Court in 1944 in the landmark decision *Smith v. Allwright*.

July 23, 2017

A tractor trailer crammed with more than one hundred immigrants is found in a Walmart parking lot. Ten died and many more were hospitalized for heatstroke and dehydration. The driver, James Bradley Jr., was sentenced to life in prison after pleading guilty to transporting the immigrants, resulting in their death.

July 24, 2002

San Antonio begins the process of adding fluoride to the public water supply. At the time it was the largest city in the country without fluoride. The proposal to add the teeth-strengthening mineral to the water system was put to voters in 1986 and fell short. On November 7, 2000, however, the fluoride referendum passed with less than 53 percent. The U.S. Centers for Disease Control and Prevention lists water fluoridation as one of the greatest public health achievements of the twentieth century.

July 25, 1820

Erasmo Seguín is sworn in as alcalde of San Antonio de Béxar. Seguín was the head of a prominent ranching family in Texas. After Mexico achieved independence from Spain, he was named Texas's sole representative to the constitutional convention, where he helped to draft the Constitution of 1824. Seguín assisted Stephen F. Austin in establishing the first colony of American settlers in Texas and later supported the Texas Revolution, providing political and material support. His son Juan was also a leader of the Texas Revolution. After the revolution, Erasmo Seguín was named a chief justice of Bexar County.

July 26, 1940

The Works Progress Administration fires thirteen employees for failure to pledge loyalty. The WPA was one of the largest New Deal agencies during the Depression, employing seventy-one thousand men in Texas to carry out public works. Thirteen workers, however, refused to sign statements that they were not Communist party members, part of a Nazi Bund, or connected to any other subversive organization. A year earlier employees who were not citizens had been removed from the rolls.

July 27, 1970

Protests begin at the San Antonio Savings Association's downtown offices over remarks Mayor Walter McAllister made in an NBC News report on San Antonio poverty.

McAllister's comments indicated his belief that Mexican Americans lacked ambition and were more concerned with "gardening." La Raza Unida called the comments "derogatory" and "racist." McAllister said his statements were taken out of context. In summer 1970 the anti-McAllister protests became a fixture in local news. He defied calls for his resignation and served out his term to 1971.

July 28, 1936

Bones and artifacts suspected of being those of the Alamo's defenders are unearthed from under the altar of San Fernando Cathedral. As a laborer shoveled beneath the cathedral floor, city officials, church leaders, and local historians watched. The story was that after the victory of San Jacinto, Juan Seguín returned to San Antonio and saw the funeral pyres from the Battle of the Alamo. He collected the remains and ashes of the defenders, placed them in a coffin, and, on February 25, 1837, gave them a military funeral burial at San Fernando. One hundred years later the rotted box was discovered, and bits of bones were collected. On May 11, 1938, they were deposited in a sarcophagus and placed on public view in the cathedral's left vestibule.

July 29, 1931

"San Antonians don't need vacations," Mayor C. M. Chambers declares. He practiced what he preached, saying he would not take one that year: "Why should I take a vacation and go anyplace, when I have Brackenridge Park and Woodlawn Lake right here beyond my own door almost?" In March 1933 Chambers died in office. C. K. Quin was appointed to complete his term.

July 30, 1982 〰〰〰〰〰〰〰〰〰〰〰〰〰〰〰〰〰〰〰

With its Spanish-Moorish architectural design, the Thomas Jefferson High School campus is named a state landmark by the Texas State Historical Society. When Jefferson was constructed in 1931, only two high schools existed in the city—Brackenridge on the South Side,

Thomas Jefferson High School, 2010

and Main Avenue on the North Side. San Antonio Independent School District purchased thirty-three acres for Jefferson in a planned housing development known as Spanish Acres. At the time it was only accessible by horseback because there were no roads past Fredericksburg Road. In 1937 Jefferson was named the Outstanding High School in America.

July 31, 1955

The San Antonio Chamber of Commerce announces a weeklong celebration for the "King of the Wild Frontier." In 1955 all things Davy Crockett were red hot, sparked by Fess Parker starring in *Davy Crockett* TV programs. San Antonio wanted its piece of this first baby boomer merchandising bonanza, and the city organized a massive Crockett birthday party with an hour-long downtown parade, a b'ar grinning contest, and plenty of coonskin caps.

AUGUST

On Susan Orlean's insistence, publishers eschewed a book jacket for her 2018 *The Library Book*. The book is bright red with gold lettering and deckle-edged pages. Orlean has said it took almost seven years for her to complete the story of the Los Angeles Public Library's Central branch, the fire of 1986 there, and the compelling mystery of the alleged arsonist, the rebuilding, and Orlean's experiences in libraries.

The book is intricately detailed, a paean to libraries, and even structured as one, with each chapter being its own volume about the library. The 1986 fire occurred at the same time Chernobyl and those terrible fires a world away were hitting American newspapers. The library fire didn't get much attention, though, until Orlean set about to investigate the story.

On June 15, 1903, San Antonio got its own library, thanks to donations of funds from steel baron Andrew Carnegie and land from the Kampmann family. Like the library in Los Angeles, San Antonio's library survived its own natural disaster. It was badly damaged in the flood of 1921 and rebuilt in an art deco style in 1930. In 1968 it became the home of the Hertzberg Circus Museum, and today the building houses the Briscoe Western Art Museum.

The first branch library of the San Antonio Public Library System opened its doors on August 5, 1930, to a large crowd. Building up the library system was a priority for Mayor C. M. Chambers. He said he wanted libraries in every corner of San Antonio, even in segregated areas. (Well worth noting is that libraries empower the disenfranchised. That certainly is the case today, even if it was difficult to perceive that in a San Antonio entrenched in de facto segregation.) Newspaper reports indicate that the following week a "Negro Library" was opened at Hackberry and Center Streets. Additional branch libraries opened soon after at Roosevelt, Woodlawn Lake Park, and Prospect Hill.

Readers voraciously devoured the libraries' offerings. In late December 1939 the library system reported that the year's most popular book had been John Steinbeck's *Grapes of Wrath*, which had a waiting list of fifty.

In July 1947 Harry Landa gave the city the deed to his home at 233 Bushnell Place. The Landa library branch established there memorializes his late wife.

San Antonio is not without its own library fire story—though it was a theoretical fire, in this case. In May 1953 Mayor Jack White proposed branding library books that had been written by Communists with warning labels. City Manager Wylie Johnson responded that it would be better to "burn the books."

The library board resisted the book-burning and labeling. But when anti-Communist book forces on the city council became the majority, the library board was replaced with a group sympathetic to their views.

Fast forward to early summer 1995 and a parade of children pulling red wagons filled with books as part of the grand opening of the "enchilada red" Central Library. The wagons carried the last books from the Main Library on Saint Mary's Street to their new home on Soledad Street.

Carl Sagan said, "I think the health of our civilization, the depth of our awareness about the underpinnings of our culture, and our concern for the future can all be tested by how well we support our libraries."

Many of us spent formative time in one or another library, in the magic of a space that belongs to everyone and can feature titles by authors ranging from "Communists" to Orlean. We recall the librarians of our youth who could be heard saying, "Shhh. Quiet now." How many of us can attest to numberless hours spent in a library, not just behind a laptop using the many digital services libraries provide? Or the necessary and fortuitous wandering through the stacks with a slip of paper containing a book's identifying Dewey Decimal number? Regardless of how you got there, or how you interact with the page—paper, electronic—when you find it, you will hug the book, or the e-reader, and go on a hunt for whatever else catches your eye.

August 1, 1931 〰〰〰〰〰〰〰〰〰〰〰〰〰〰〰〰〰〰〰〰

The San Antonio School Board announces that due to the Depression married women will receive low priority in the hiring of new teachers. The following June all married women whose husbands earned a minimum $2,000 annual salary were terminated. In 1931 the Bexar County courthouse offices began dismissing married women. Even the pro-union *San Antonio Dispatch* newspaper supported the spurious argument that a man has a greater claim to a job than a woman.

August 2, 1977 〰〰〰〰〰〰〰〰〰〰〰〰〰〰〰〰〰〰〰〰

Congressman Henry B. González calls for changes to the Constitution's presidential succession amendment. The

Mural of Henry B. González

Twenty-Fifth Amendment was ratified by Congress in 1967 to lay out who takes over the executive branch if the president is incapacitated or deemed unfit to lead. The amendment has been used only once to permanently replace a president—Richard Nixon. González warned that the amendment was not adequate to deal with "possible tests it might encounter, no matter how bizarre."

August 3, 1974

After an eleven-day prison break attempt, San Antonio drug kingpin Fred Gómez Carrasco dies in a shootout in Huntsville. Carrasco and two other inmates had obtained smuggled pistols and took hostages in the prison library. Over the next eleven days they made demands for such things as tailored suits, dress shoes, and cologne. The convicts tried to dash to a waiting car by building a shield of law books taped together into a tank, which the press called the "Trojan Taco." Two hostages were killed in the ensuing gun battle, and Carrasco took his own life at the scene.

August 4, 1891

The "Bawdy House Ordinance" legalizing and licensing houses of prostitution goes into effect. The city clerk saw brisk business immediately, with four houses licensed that same day. The "houses of ill-fame" were required to pay $300 a year to operate, and the city physician would inspect houses for sanitation. According to the *Daily Light*, "Only the big land ladies can afford to pay the license. The smaller fry will have to quit town, dodge the law, cajole the officers, or form a community for the payment of the tax." A week later the newspaper reported that police had arrested twenty-five "unfortunate women" for violating the ordinance. They were told to pay the $25 fine and get a license or leave the city, and if they could not pay the fine they would be jailed for twenty-five days. Male clients of bawds were not subject to licensing, restrictions, or legal ramifications.

August 5, 1930

The San Pedro library, the city's first branch, has its grand opening. A large crowd turned out to view the library, with its elegant Spanish-style architecture and vaulted ceiling. This was a busy time for the San Antonio library system, which was a priority for Mayor C. M. Chambers. The Main Library at Market and Presa Streets had reopened earlier that week after extensive renovations following flooding and after closing a temporary location in the Municipal Auditorium basement. The following week a "Negro Library" was opened at Hackberry and Center Streets. That same week the Roosevelt branch opened, followed in September by branches at Woodlawn Lake Park and Prospect Hill. Chambers said he wanted libraries to be available in every corner of San Antonio.

August 6, 1955

A claim that Mexican revolutionary Pancho Villa hid a stash of gold in San Antonio is met with little excitement. From her sickbed, an elderly Dolores Vasquez told an Associated Press reporter that she had fought in Villa's army and had helped bury $1.5 million in gold coins in a local churchyard with high walls and an orange tree. She said she couldn't claim the treasure herself because people would wonder why an old woman had all those gold coins. San Antonio police said that despite the story there was no sign of a public treasure hunt.

August 7, 1954

Lackland Air Force trainee Johnny Cash marries Vivian Liberto at Saint Ann's Catholic Church. He was nineteen years old, and she was seventeen. Their courtship included many strolls along the River Walk, where Cash carved "Johnny Loves Vivian" into a cedar bench, now on display at the Witte Museum. Later Cash penned the song "I Walk the Line" about his devotion to Liberto. In his song "Folsom Prison Blues" a guilt-ridden prisoner dreams of returning to San Antonio. Liberto filed for divorce in 1966, citing Cash's drug abuse and his many affairs, including one with June Carter, whom Cash eventually married.

August 8, 1987

Joske's department store rings up its last transaction. Generations of San Antonians made the trip to the store for an extravagant day of shopping and childhood wonderment. Founded in 1867 by German immigrant Julius Joske, the five-story flagship at Alamo and Commerce Streets opened in 1887 and eventually became the largest department store west of the Mississippi and the first in Texas to be air-conditioned and to install escalators. After many protests, it was one of the city's last public places to accept integration. The store fell victim to corporate buyouts and closed in 1987.

August 9, 1950

Mayor Jack White vetoes a resolution passed by city commissioners calling for a December 19 charter election. White said the date had been deliberately selected to hurt the cause of charter reform: "This is a cunning, clever attempt to deceive our people and strangle their growing determination to improve local government." He called the charter election for May 9, but with too many amendments on a ballot and dissension within the pro-city manager ranks it failed to pass. On August 9, 1951, the Charter Review Commission headed by Walter McAllister presented a 165-section council-manager charter proposal, which voters passed by a margin of nearly two to one on October 2. This was the long-sought victory in the fight to install a city manager government model, started in 1939 by business leaders who wanted to bring transparency and good government to city hall.

August 10, 1862

In what will become known as the Nueces Massacre, Confederate lieutenant C. D. McRea leads a San Antonio detachment of ninety-four men to intercept sixty-four German Texans fleeing to Mexico. The Germans, from Kendall, Kerr, and Gillespie Counties, were planning to go to New Orleans to join the Union army. The Confederacy saw these men as deserters. McRea tracked them to the Nueces River and attacked. Most were killed in the raid, and the wounded were executed. The seven survivors were taken back to Gillespie County and hanged. A monument to the fallen stands in Comfort, Texas.

August 11, 1915

Because of residents' increased interest in river bathing, the city finds it necessary to create a new swimming hole. Lambert Beach at Brackenridge Park had become insufficient to accommodate the throngs looking to cool off. To create a "beach" the city cleared weeds and rubbish from the San Antonio River at Guenther Street and dumped a truckload of sand along the riverbank. Lights were installed for night swimming, and a bathhouse was constructed.

August 12, 1954 //

Another city manager is fired. Mayor Jack "Boss" White declared that City Manager Ralph Winton had to go. This came as a surprise to many, including Winton, who had held the job for about a year and brought the city into a budget surplus. Winton was the fourth city manager under the city manager government model, adopted two years earlier. The public was outraged, and there was an immediate recall petition drive for Mayor White and the four councilmembers who supported him. *San Antonio Express-News* reporter Paul Thompson called it "San Antonio's zaniest and most explosive political week of all time." White resigned several days later, and for the next six months San Antonio politics was thrown into chaos.

August 13, 1922 //

A border shootout erupts over contraband. Two years into Prohibition, San Antonio, known at the time as Little Chicago, had become a hub for outlawed booze and gangsters, bootleggers, and smugglers. The city customs office reported that tequila smugglers were stopped as they attempted to cross the Rio Grande between Del Rio and Eagle Pass. A running gun battle that killed two horses used as pack animals ensued. The smugglers fled back across the border into Mexico and escaped the agents in the dark of night.

August 14, 1922 〰〰〰〰〰〰〰〰〰〰〰〰〰〰〰〰〰〰〰〰

The Bexar County town of Viva is wiped off the map. Viva was established in 1887 as a flag stop town for steam engines heading to Kerrville on the San Antonio–Aransas Pass Railroad. It had grown to include a depot, a general store, and a number of houses, with children attending school in nearby Leon Springs. Viva languished and finally ceased to exist that morning in August when county judge James R. Davis signed a petition that ordered the streets and alleys of the town closed.

August 15, 1745 〰〰〰〰〰〰〰〰〰〰〰〰〰〰〰〰〰〰〰〰

After thirty years of bloody conflict, Captain Toribio de Urrutia brokers peace with the Apache Nation. That morning a cavernous hole was dug in Main Plaza, and a throng of people gathered to witness what came next. In the hole were placed a hatchet, a lance, six arrows, and a live horse. Urrutia and four chiefs joined hands and danced three times around the hole. Then priests, soldiers, citizens, and Indians did the same. A signal was given, and the hole was quickly filled in. The weapons were buried along with the horse, bringing an end to the war.

August 16, 1955

Audie Murphy arrives in San Antonio for the world premiere of his film *To Hell and Back* at the Majestic Theatre the following evening. The Texas-born, baby-faced celebrity was America's most decorated soldier in World War II, receiving twenty-one medals including the Medal of Honor. Murphy played himself in the movie, which tells the story of his combat heroism and how he single-handedly held off an entire company of German soldiers. Downtown streets were jam-packed for a parade in Murphy's honor.

August 17, 1987

San Antonio police officer Farrell Tucker learns that fellow officer Stephen Smith is planning to murder Bexar County district attorney Sam Millsap along with other members of the police department. Smith had been indicted for beating a shoplifting suspect and was furious about his perceived betrayal by the police department. The following day Tucker told officials of Smith's plan, and they instructed Tucker to meet with Smith that night and secretly record a confession. Things took a deadly turn. Smith pulled a gun, but Tucker shot first. Later it was revealed that Smith was likely responsible for a number of other violent acts targeting San Antonio police.

Audie Murphy, 1948

August 18, 1813

The Battle of Medina is fought approximately twenty miles south of San Antonio de Béxar as part of the Mexican War of Independence. The Spanish Royalist army was victorious against fourteen hundred local troops supporting the Republic; the troops included Anglos, Tejanos, Indians, and former Royalists. After a four-hour battle, only about a hundred Republicans managed to escape being killed or captured. Two days later the Spanish army entered San Antonio to brutally punish the civilian population. That night is remembered as La Noche Triste. Seven hundred citizens were imprisoned, and eighteen of the three hundred held in the granary on Main Plaza died of suffocation. Executions were held in Military Plaza the next day.

August 19, 1935

Mayor C. K. Quin orders murals, alleged to contain hidden pro-Communist symbols, removed from Municipal Auditorium. The local chapter of the American Legion complained that the murals were of a sinister nature and proved that Communists had penetrated San Antonio, much like Mexican painter Diego Rivera had at Rockefeller Center in New York. Painted by Xavier Gonzalez, the murals included the image of an upraised fist and a palm with bleeding wounds. Gonzalez later moved to New York City to paint. His works are in the collections of the Metropolitan Museum of Art and many other museums.

August 20, 1906 〜〜〜〜〜〜〜〜〜〜〜〜〜〜〜〜〜〜〜〜〜〜〜〜〜

The city council passes an ordinance regulating the burial of persons who have died from various contagious and infectious diseases. Under the ordinance, it was unlawful for any undertaker to have a public burial of someone who died of typhoid fever, typhus fever, measles, small-pox, diphtheria, cholera, typho-malaria, yellow fever, plague, epidemic cerebrospinal meningitis, or glanders. Anyone in charge of the burial of a person who died from these diseases was required to report it to the Board of Health.

August 21, 1937 〜〜〜〜〜〜〜〜〜〜〜〜〜〜〜〜〜〜〜〜〜〜〜〜〜〜〜

The city's slum clearance director announces that 825 West Side shacks will be destroyed. The action was the result of a city drive to eliminate the Mexican American shantytown and clear land for development. Under the U.S. Housing Act of 1937, federal funds were available for housing programs, but San Antonio's response was controversial and ruled ineligible for the money. That changed in 1939 after First Lady Eleanor Roosevelt saw the housing conditions firsthand and declared the city's slums some of the worst she'd ever witnessed. She then worked to bring public housing programs to the West Side.

August 22, 1928 \\\

Leita Small, the official custodian of the Alamo, reports that tourists won't stop carving their names into the walls of the Texas shrine. Small signs were posted asking visitors to resist the temptation to whittle into the historic structure, but they were immediately stolen as souvenirs. Small claimed that she tried to keep a watchful eye on tourists, but as soon as her back was turned, out came the pocketknives. The visiting vandals were also cutting chunks out of the Alamo's doors to take home a piece of Texas history.

August 23, 1970 \\\

A Led Zeppelin concert in San Antonio is canceled due to an outbreak of diphtheria. More than fifty thousand people were inoculated in the span of ten days to slow the spread of the mounting epidemic. The diagnosis of fifty-four local cases spurred the health department to declare an emergency and open an immunization clinic. Most cases were in the city's poorer Mexican American neighborhoods. A spokesperson from the War on Poverty Agency said they were authorized to spend $15,000 for the emergency clinics. The city health department urged San Antonio Independent School District to adopt a tougher immunization policy; at the time only the smallpox vaccination was required.

August 24, 1935

Texans go to the polls to vote on a state constitutional amendment ending Prohibition. Two years earlier Prohibition had been repealed nationally, but that had no effect in Texas because of the 1919 state prohibition amendment. Proposition 1 would end Prohibition in Texas in 1935 but still prohibit "open saloons" and allow local governments to decide if they would be wet or dry. There was no doubt that San Antonio would be a wet city. Bexar County had the largest margin of victory for the repeal, six to one.

August 25, 1939

Five thousand protesters storm Municipal Auditorium when labor leader Emma Tenayuca attempts to hold a Communist Party meeting. Tenayuca, a leading controversial figure, had successfully led a strike of local pecan shellers. The day of the meeting trucks with loudspeakers roamed the streets decrying Tenayuca as "un-American." It was clear there was going to be trouble, and in preparation the entire police department was assembled for crowd control and the emergency room was double-staffed. The crowd, which included members of the Ku Klux Klan, hurled bricks at police officers, and the police responded with tear gas and firehoses. The mob was undeterred and burned in effigy Mayor Maury Maverick, who recognized Tenayuca's right to freedom of speech and had granted the permit for the event. The auditorium was set on fire to drive Tenayuca out to be lynched. Police officers managed to smuggle her from the building undetected through a secret passage. She fled the city and didn't return for almost thirty years.

August 26, 1971

High hopes for a San Antonio–Austin regional airport are terminated when the city council is briefed that the Federal Aviation Administration will not support the ambitious plan. Congressman Henry B. González had been a booster for a shared airport. San Antonio leaders were enthusiastic, saying there was an urgent need to replace the current international airport, but Austin leaders were reluctant to embrace the plan, which called for the airport to be located about twenty miles north of San Antonio in New Braunfels. Austin officials saw that as too far south to effectively benefit the capital city.

August 27, 1966

More than a hundred Rio Grande Valley farmworkers on a protest march enter San Antonio. The laborers began their three-hundred-mile trek on July 4 and had planned to end on Labor Day at the state capitol. They were seeking a state minimum wage of $1.25 an hour and clean drinking water and bathrooms at their work sites. The marchers gathered in the pouring rain at Main Plaza and then attended mass at San Fernando Cathedral celebrated by Archbishop Robert Lucey.

August 28, 1937

Mayor C. K. Quin declares the chili queens a public health nuisance and bans them from Market Square and other public areas. For more than one hundred years San Antonio's plazas were populated with the smells, tastes, and sounds of these unique open-air food vendors, who were known for their beauty and charm as well as their culinary offerings. But in 1937 with an election looming Mayor C. K. Quin made the chili queens an issue. The dishes and recipes they invented were the forerunners of the Tex-Mex food industry.

August 29, 1936

City auditor Walter Tatsch stays busy counting nickels after the city's first full day of parking meter use. Police were out in force to help drivers navigate the 370 devices, which were an unwelcome novelty for downtown shoppers. One nickel bought the maximum time of one hour at a space on Commerce Street. The plan was to install fifteen hundred meters downtown. Shopkeepers complained that they would hurt their trade, since few customers would want to pay for parking.

August 30, 2008

The Eagle Ford Shale boom begins. Conventional wisdom declared South Texas tapped out for oil, and skeptics scoffed at Petrohawk's plan for an experimental fracking well drilled in La Salle County. But when the well began to produce, a land rush kicked off that would pump billions of dollars of wealth to the region and more than a billion barrels of oil for an energy-hungry nation. While a debate can be had about the environmental cost

of fracking, there's no denying that it created fortunes and changed life in South Texas.

August 31, 1939 〰〰〰〰〰〰〰〰〰〰〰〰〰〰〰〰〰〰〰〰〰〰〰〰

Sweeping changes are made to the city's garbage system. A survey of the rubbish arrangement found that two of the city's incinerators needed replacing. The method of garbage disposal was deemed obsolete, and the incinerator at Brackenridge Park was pointed out as particularly bothersome; it would have to be abandoned when the municipal stadium was built. In addition, the incinerator at Travis and Las Moras Streets, which delivered smoke into the densely populated neighborhood, was a health hazard. Mayor Maury Maverick recommended that the city find a suitable place for a garbage dump.

SEPTEMBER

n the late eighteenth century the United States was poised at the threshold of developments in modern science but experienced a collective, relentless drumbeat of pain. There was little to quell discomfort and disease. Diarists of the time, including Benjamin Franklin, described the capricious nature of pain.

Over the course of its three-hundred-year history, San Antonio has seen the discovery of anesthesia in the 1840s, aspirin in the 1890s, and antibiotics in the 1920s, and its citizens have been able to control pain to a large extent. These advances that began in the 1800s coincide with the notions of rationalism and the realism art movement, which could in some way have heightened sensitivity to anxiety or agony—the byproducts of pain. But there is nothing in the rhetoric of the time to suggest that people were less susceptible to the idea of pain as influential in its power to control people, besides just moving them toward adapting to pain or fighting against it.

On September 3, 1866, San Antonio experienced a cholera outbreak. Two hundred ninety-two people succumbed to the effects of the illness, a bacterial disease that spreads through contaminated water. It was the second cholera epidemic in less than two decades: an epidemic in 1849 had killed five hundred. With the later outbreak, remedy came in the form of proactive reforms in the city infrastructure. Sidewalks were paved and street gutters installed to move and drain stagnant water.

Early American ministers preached that pain was the punishment for original sin. God meted out pain to test the faithful or punish them for transgressions. Modern medicine can prevent or alleviate pain, at least to an extent. So religious explanations of the origin of pain or the reason for it were replaced by Americans' logic that what could not be controlled was abnormal. Furthermore, how should we account for the outbreak of cholera—or influenza or diphtheria, in the case of San Antonio—if correctives to city infrastructure, not divine intervention, stemmed the tide of these rampant epidemics?

In her seminal 2005 essay "The Pain Scale," Eula Biss writes that there are four vital signs to determine a patient's health: blood pressure, temperature, breathing, and pulse. "Recently," she writes, "it has been suggested that pain be considered a fifth vital sign."

We've all seen the Wong-Baker FACES pain rating scale in the doctor's office or hospital room or some article we landed on after a late-night internet search of nagging symptoms. It looks like a precursor to the emoji and was developed to help young children rate their pain if they lacked a lexicon to describe it.

Biss writes about seeing an article on the front page of a newspaper. A wildfire had destroyed the house of a man pictured in the story: "The man's face was horrifyingly distorted in an open-mouthed cry of raw pain. But the man himself, the article reveals, had not been hurt." The moment leads her to an understanding about human suffering, pain that is real and visceral but cannot be identified on the body. If we cannot point to the pain, what lengths will we go to make the suffering stop?

In *Regarding the Pain of Others*, Susan Sontag explains how images—precisely like the photo of the man Biss references—that move us closer to the idea of pain fail to connect us fully. She asserts that no image can truly depict the reality of war, devastation, and suffering. We can stare at an image but can never know the pain fully. Reading history or watching the news can become a voyeuristic act. "Remembering is an ethical act," Sontag writes, and it "has ethical value in and of itself." If we do nothing after the remembering, we are cruel: "Heartlessness and amnesia seem to go together. But history gives contradictory signals about the value of remembering in the much longer span of a collective history. There is simply too much injustice in the world."

Throughout history, pain has reinforced the idea of human fragility. Controlling pain was equal to power. Letting pain dominate reflected weakness, inferiority.

On May 30, 1858, four men were hanged from a tree near Mission San José. The four were Mexican. Their names were Francisco Huizan, Pablo Longoria, Felipe Lopez, and Nicanor Urdiales. Without evidence or due process, a secret vigilante group had accused the four men of stealing horses and lynched them.

What a gruesome image emerges in the mind's eye. Texas history is full of lynching victims who were black, Mexican, Mexican American, Native American—victims numbering in the hundreds. San Antonio had its share of such acts. We should remember this part of our painful past.

Sontag wrote that "to make peace is to forget. To reconcile, it is necessary that memory be faulty and limited. If the goal is having some space in which to live one's own life, then it is desirable that the account of specific injustices dissolve into a more general understanding that human beings everywhere do terrible things to one another."

We can turn away, change the channel, move the needle of our vicarious pain scale to zero, but that action can never remove what an image—or story—conveys. Denizens of a city make an implicit pact with their neighbors. If we are susceptible to illness and pain because of proximity, we have likewise entered into a contract to help each other resolve our problems. It is our responsibility—for sharing common rights and observing the same laws—to help alleviate each other's pain. Our empathic intentions should be infectious. What is a city if not a collection of people brought together by dint of destiny to do just that?

September 1, 2017

San Antonio's monument to Confederate soldiers is taken down. The city council voted ten to one in favor of removal after public outcry. The Daughters of the Confederacy erected the statue of an unnamed Confederate soldier facing south and pointing to the sky in Travis Park in 1900. Opponents of the monument claimed it honored those who rebelled against the United States and fought to preserve slavery. For generations the monument and others like it across the nation have been seen as reminders of the brutal horrors of Jim Crow and racial inequalities that persist in the South.

September 2, 1964

The Bexar County Medical Society denies paying for telegrams opposing Medicare. The day before, on September 1, Congressman Henry B. González revealed that he had received 214 telegrams from local doctors, dentists, and nurses pleading with him to fight against passage of a bill that would provide medical care for the elderly under the Social Security system. The medical society argued that Medicare wasn't necessary because local doctors frequently provided free or discounted medical treatment to the elderly. González said the barrage of telegrams was the most he had ever received opposing a bill in Congress. On July 30, 1965, President Lyndon B.

Johnson signed legislation establishing the Medicare and Medicaid programs.

September 3, 1866 〰〰〰〰〰〰〰〰〰〰〰〰〰〰〰〰〰〰〰

A cholera outbreak begins in San Antonio, eventually claiming 292 lives. Cholera is a bacterial disease, usually spread through contaminated water, which causes severe diarrhea and dehydration. It can be fatal in a matter of hours, even in otherwise healthy people. The previous San Antonio cholera epidemic, in 1849, lasted six weeks and killed some five hundred. Word of a new outbreak caused people to flee the city in fear. To prevent future outbreaks the Board of Health recommended reforms such as paving sidewalks and grading streets to provide gutters that would drain stagnant waters.

September 4, 1942 〰〰〰〰〰〰〰〰〰〰〰〰〰〰〰〰〰〰〰〰

The hospital at Fort Sam Houston is designated Brooke Army Hospital in recognition of Gen. Roger Brooke, who entered the U.S. Army Medical Corps in 1901 and became a specialist in infectious diseases, later serving as commanding officer of the Fort Sam hospital from 1928 to 1933. The hospital's roots go back to 1870, when the post was established in San Antonio and the medical facility was a small log cabin. Today Brooke Army Medical Center leads the world in almost every aspect of health care and medical treatment, training, and research.

September 5, 1938

San Antonio recognizes Labor Day with a two-day celebration and a parade through downtown of two thousand workers representing thirty-one unions and organizations. While the nation was in the grips of the Depression, workers' rights took on added significance. Members of different unions marched in their working clothes with pride. There was a picnic at San Pedro Park with pro-labor speeches, band music, and a softball game between the women workers of Pearl Brewery (the "Brewetts") and the Bat Corrigans.

September 6, 1861

Bob Augustin is arrested for disorderly conduct—specifically, wrecking the chili stands of Main Plaza. Augustin rode into town from Goliad to join Sibley's Brigade, an ill-fated Confederacy plan organized in San Antonio to invade the New Mexico territory. Two days after Augustin's arrest he was released from jail, but he was taken by a lynch mob that brought him to the hanging tree, La Ley de Mondragon, at the southeast corner of Military Plaza. The mob declared by unanimous consent that Augustin was a "bad man."

September 7, 1926

The motion picture *Wings* begins filming in San Antonio. Another Hollywood silent movie, *The Rough Riders*,

Wings movie poster, 1927

was also shooting in town. The scrubland of Camp Bullis stood in for Cuba's San Juan Hill, while a battle-scarred "French Village" was constructed at Camp Stanley for *Wings*. During those months Hollywood's biggest stars occupied the city, including Clara Bow, Mary Astor, Gary Cooper, and Hedda Hopper. Hundreds of local extras were needed for the filming, as were pilots, planes, and explosives supplied by the U.S. military. *Wings* received the first Oscar for best picture.

September 8, 1943

A citywide blackout doesn't go as planned. San Antonio's air raid Civil Defense staged a war exercise. At 9:45 p.m. an air siren sounded, and citizens had been instructed to turn lights off so they wouldn't be an easy target for enemy bombardiers. Instead the local population essentially ignored the Klaxon. According to newspaper reports, many were confused and others didn't take the drill seriously; several hoodlum gangs, however, took it upon themselves to enforce the blackout and broke neon signs by hurling stones.

September 9, 1921

The Great Flood hits the city after the remnants of a hurricane dump approximately thirteen inches of rain in the Olmos Basin, causing flash floods and at least fifty-two deaths. A wall of water ten to thirty inches high tore through downtown and into area creeks, flooding

Saint Mary's Church rectory entrance, 1921

downstream neighborhoods. The San Antonio River was transformed into a torrent of uncontrolled water two miles wide. There was widespread damage. Houses were lifted from their foundations and piled on one another. Cattle were impaled on fence posts, and vehicles were overturned. Bridges were swept away. Military forces at Fort Sam Houston and Camp Travis cooperated in relief and policing with the city and county officers and patrolled downtown to prevent looting. A temporary morgue was established at the Central Fire and Police Station where bodies could be brought for identification.

The flooding occurred across south-central Texas and took an estimated 250 lives.

September 10, 1970 ///

Walter McAllister stirs controversy as his comments about Mexican Americans continue to provoke contention in the city council chambers. In an interview airing on NBC's *Huntley-Brinkley Report*, Mayor McAllister was asked about the violence at a Los Angeles protest march and commented that "our Mexicans" prefer to sing and dance. They were "not ambitiously motivated as the Anglos to get ahead financially." There were immediate calls for the mayor to apologize, but he refused. Protests and pickets were organized outside his downtown bank, San Antonio Savings Association. Councilman Pete Torres challenged McAllister's claim that the comments were "taken out of context." The day before, at a protest in front of San Antonio Savings, twenty-seven people were arrested for disturbing the peace, including county commissioner Albert Peña Jr. and East Side leader Rev. G. J. Sutton. Peña told the press that McAllister was "a Nazi, a Fascist, or both." The protests and a boycott continued, and eventually McAllister apologized.

September 11, 1890 ///

The U.S. War Department designates San Antonio military post Fort Sam Houston in honor of Gen. Sam

Houston. When it was established in 1845, it was called simply the post at San Antonio. In the 1870s it started construction and land acquisition, and by 1891 it was the army's second-largest post. It played a critical role in protecting the region during the Indian conflicts, securing the Mexican border, military aviation, and training and deployment during the world wars.

September 12, 1912

The project to widen Commerce Street begins. As automobiles took over, it became clear that the city's Wall Street was too narrow for streetcars and Model Ts. During the four-year street-widening project many of San Antonio's notable bullet-riddled and battle-scarred structures were demolished. The new five-story Alamo National Bank was physically raised, put on rollers, and moved back seventeen feet, while banking operations continued uninterrupted.

September 13, 1987

Pope John Paul II is welcomed in San Antonio with mariachi music and the gift of a cowboy hat. The popular pontiff paraded in front of the Alamo in the popomobile and celebrated at least three services. One was for parishioners at Our Lady of Guadalupe church on the West Side. More than 250,000 attended mass near Westover Hills. In his homily, the pope spoke about needs along the U.S.-Mexico border; he called San Antonio a crossroads and said it was our duty to show mercy to people moving northward from Mexico.

September 14, 1915 //

The city council warns local Mexican Americans that anti-American, inflammatory, or anarchistic speeches will not be tolerated at the celebration of Mexican independence. The city issued the order as Mexico was in the grips of a revolution. Relations with the United States were so bad that there was an embargo on crossing the border by Mexicans. San Antonio leaders granted local Mexicans the use of San Pedro Park, but no disorder would be tolerated. They were concerned that cross-border revolutionaries would try to stir up trouble.

September 15, 1968 //

One person is killed and forty-seven others are injured after two HemisFair monorail trains collide. As one train rounded a curve its brakes failed and it struck the other train from behind. Both monorails derailed, and the cars and passengers fell twelve feet into a lagoon. The one-and-a-half-mile monorail was one of the signature attractions of HemisFair, which closed operations on October 6. The monorail was used to transport more than one million attendees during the fair's run.

September 16, 1937

Mayor C. K. Quin tells the Bexar County grand jury to indict Owen P. White, author of "Machine Made," which appeared in *Collier's*, for libel. The article described graft, political corruption, and election rigging that controlled San Antonio and Bexar County. Quin was singled out as an individual who profited from gambling operations, prostitution shakedowns, and ballot harvesting. He read parts of the article to the grand jury and pointed out the sections that he thought were particularly libelous. Criminal libel, however, is a misdemeanor and not an offense for which the writer could be extradited. The grand jury reportedly responded that they would seek more facts about the case, but no charges were ever produced. On December 31 the grand jury issued its final report, calling for a full independent investigation by the U.S. Public Health Service into the city's health department.

September 17, 1842

The Battle of Salado Creek repels a Mexican invasion. After Texas independence there was the continued threat of Mexico trying to reconquer lost territory. In August 1842 the Mexican army crossed the Rio Grande looking to regain Texas. Republic forces were overwhelmed and fell back to regroup. Col. Mathew Caldwell led just over two hundred Texicans against sixteen hundred Mexican soldiers and Cherokee warriors outside San Antonio, along Salado Creek. He drew the Mexican troops into a trap along the creek bed. The battle lasted five hours, with Texican sharpshooters doing most of the damage to the Mexican line. Then Mexican troops were ordered to charge the Texican position. Although they had vastly superior numbers the Mexicans were driven back, and when night came they quietly retreated. This was a decisive and significant victory for the Republic of Texas.

September 18, 1842

The dead from the Dawson Massacre are discovered the day after the victory of Salado Creek. Col. Mathew Caldwell and his militia find the bodies of slain men who had joined the battle. A company of fifty-four Texicans, mostly from Fayette County, under the command of Nicholas Mosby Dawson had answered the call for reinforcements, attacking the Mexican army's rear. The Mexicans counterattacked with five hundred cavalry officers and two cannons. Once the cannons opened fire, Dawson's militia began suffering numerous casualties. Dawson tried to surrender by waving a white jacket, but the Mexican forces refused to yield and continued their barrage. According to Texas lore, Dawson's dying words were "let victory be purchased with blood."

September 19, 1837

San Antonio elects its first mayor since independence from Mexico. John William Smith won in a landslide—all of fifteen votes. Smith twice served as a messenger during the siege of the Alamo and was known around town as El Colorado, a Spanish nickname for a redhead. As mayor, he prohibited public bathing in the San Antonio River and San Pedro Creek between the hours of 5 a.m. and 8 p.m. He also allowed cows to roam downtown as long as they were milked and back in the corral before 10 p.m.

September 20, 1885

San Antonio adopts a six-shooter ordinance that requires everyone—even police officers—to get a permit to carry a hip cannon. City officials promised they would strictly enforce the ordinance, and they did. Three weeks later Cliff Cook, a gambler, was at the White Elephant Saloon and attempted to terrorize the barkeeper with his six-shooter. In doing so, he frightened the men and women out into the street. He was collared by a Captain Fowler and fined $50. It was common for laws to be passed criminalizing the possession and sale of certain guns in the Wild West era.

September 21, 1925

With an enrollment of two hundred, San Antonio College formally opens its doors as University Junior College, with classes conducted at the old Main High School building. San Antonio College is the state's oldest public two-year college still in operation. When it opened, the school was part of the University of Texas system, but three months later the state attorney general ruled the arrangement unconstitutional. The San Antonio Board of Education took over the college, and in 1945 the San Antonio Union Junior College District was established. The name was changed to the Alamo Colleges District in 1982.

September 22, 1954

Recall petitions for three city councilmembers and the mayor are certified by the city clerk, but before a recall election date can be set the councilmembers quickly adjourn the meeting and flee the chambers. More than nineteen thousand petition signatures were gathered for the recall elections of Mayor R. L. Lester, R. N. "Dick" White Jr., R. V. "Ralph" Easley, and Mrs. Thelma Stevens. Under the city charter a recall election must be called in thirty to forty days. But after a series of rapid-fire resignations, forced appointment votes, and council meeting shouting matches, city politics was plunged into a period of instability akin to the theater of the absurd. Lester became mayor when Jack "Boss" White resigned in scandal and served as mayor for thirty days, from September 9 to October 20. When the dust settled on May 1, 1955, a new elected council was sworn in and the twenty-year era of relative stability with the Good Government League began.

September 23, 1924 ~~~~~~

Standing behind a team of mules with his hands on a plow, Mayor John W. Tobin breaks ground for the city auditorium. The auditorium was part of a $5 million downtown improvement initiative that included new bridges and flood control projects. Voters approved two bond elections for the auditorium in 1919 and 1923, and a third would be required before its dedication on September 3, 1926. Municipal Auditorium was dedicated to all San Antonio men who gave their lives in military service. At that time the building was also seen as a monument to the service of Mayor Tobin. Today it is the site of the Tobin Center for the Performing Arts, named for Robert Lynn Batts Tobin, a philanthropist and devotee of the arts.

September 24, 1839 ~~~~~~

John Leonard Riddell, a physician, geologist, and botanist, arrives in San Antonio. Riddell was on an expedition to find the lost silver mine of San Saba. He didn't find it, but he did record his keen observations in his book *A Long Ride in Texas*. He found a lawless frontier that was being fought over by Anglo settlers, Native tribes, Mexican forces, and murderous outlaws of every stripe. In

John Leonard Riddell

San Antonio, Riddell wrote about the community of La Villita, with its adobe huts with reeds for thatched roofs.

September 25, 1929 //

A deadly ambush awaits prohibition officer Capt. Charles Stevens. The pitched gun battle between the dry agents and the bootleggers happened on Pleasanton Road after midnight. Earlier that night the agents had uncovered the city's largest illegal distillery, which was operated by the moonshine king of San Antonio, Lynn Stephens, who wanted revenge and set a trap to attack the agents. He fled to Mexico and hid out for twenty years. Broke and ill from a ruptured ulcer, Stephens eventually surrendered and was given thirty-eight years in prison.

September 26, 1948

President Harry Truman's whistle-stop campaign pulls into San Antonio. The cross-country tour resulted in his upset defeat of odds-on favorite Thomas E. Dewey. Truman attended Sunday service at the First Baptist Church and toured the Old Governor's Palace and the Alamo. That night he gave a dinner speech before guests that included House Speaker Sam Rayburn. Truman said Rayburn was a "hard-shell Baptist" and Truman was a "lightfoot Baptist," but he couldn't explain the difference given that he was speaking on the Sabbath.

September 27, 1833

Lt. Francisco de Castañeda and one hundred Mexican dragoons leave San Antonio and head to Gonzales to retrieve a cannon. The bronze six-pounder was given to settlers in 1831 for protection from frequent Comanche raids. But the citizens refused to give up the cannon and hastily prepared a flag—now a popular icon—with an image of a cannon and the words "Come and Take It." Castañeda found himself outmanned and outgunned and returned to San Antonio empty-handed. The Battle of Gonzales is considered the first battle of the Texas Revolution.

September 28, 1931 〰〰〰〰〰〰〰〰〰〰〰〰〰〰〰〰〰〰〰〰

The Depression brings ruin to a big bank. The financial crisis forced one-third of San Antonio's twenty-one financial institutions into insolvency, but the failure of City Central Bank and Trust Company was especially devastating. In "Beyond Denial: Glimpses of Depression-Era San Antonio," which appeared in the *South Texas Historical Journal*, L. Patrick Hughes wrote that it took a year, but the firm eventually reemerged as South Texas Bank and Trust. In the meantime depositors, including the city, had no access to even a portion of their funds. The impact on the local economy and municipal government was extreme and incalculable. The Federal Deposit Insurance Corporation had not yet been formed, so depositors' money wasn't protected.

September 29, 1938 〰〰〰〰〰〰〰〰〰〰〰〰〰〰〰〰〰〰〰〰

During a House Un-American Activities Committee hearing, an undercover investigator testifies that San Antonio is a hub for German American Bund members. The Bund was an American pro-Nazi organization consisting of Americans of German descent with the goal of promoting a favorable view of Nazi Germany. The agent testified that in fall 1937 he met with a Bund official in San Antonio who was a secret agent of the German government. He said the secret agent expressed frustration with the Texas German population who were unwilling to join his cause and quoted the Bund official as saying, "You know the German American people of Texas don't respond to that sort of thing." During World War II a total of 11,507 people of German ancestry were arrested and sent to internment camps.

September 30, 1937

Marble boards, pinball, and dice games remain in place near local schools despite a campaign to oust them from the city. Mayor C. K. Quin and the school board had declared a war against the "nickel grabbers," saying the machines had a hold on youth and were training them to become gamblers. The head of the San Antonio PTA complained that children were spending their lunch money on the machines and not getting sufficient nutrition. The city commission issued an order to all places of business in the city to stop minors from playing the games. A similar order had been issued earlier, but it was not strictly enforced. The mayor's office warned that violating businesses would have their machines confiscated.

OCTOBER

n his autobiography, Benjamin Franklin relates his escape from poverty in a large family in Boston as a means of conveying his ascent as an enlightened man of the world. This sweeping allegorical tale is the story of one man, but it is also the story of the United States.

Yet for all its depth and breadth, the work, which is considered one of the most important autobiographies ever written, never mentions Franklin's sister Jane. She considered him her "second self." He was the youngest of the ten sons in the Franklin family, and she was the youngest of the seven daughters. They were called Benny and Jenny, and it was roundly considered that no other two members of that expansive family were more alike.

Historian Jill Lepore believes that Jane's story is also an allegory: "It explains what it means to write history not from what survives but from what is lost." Jane saved her brother's letters written over decades. The letters she wrote to him are long gone. All we know is that they do not exist. Even in this stark way, he so much as erased her, even if unwittingly.

When Jane set about to write her own book, it was rough-hewn one she stitched together out of foolscap and thick twine. In her "Book of Ages" she recorded the births and deaths of her children. It was, as Lepore characterizes it, "a litany of grief." While Benjamin explored the rest of the world, Jane never left Boston, hardly left her house, and didn't have her own room until she was sixty-nine.

Lepore discovered in the dearth of those pages, the dates of births and deaths, a deeper story. Benjamin Franklin's omissions of his sister in his life story manage to tell the story of her obscurity, her quiet tending to others at the sacrifice of what she loved as much as her brother did—books. In other words, the omission is the inclusion. "The facts of Jane Franklin's life are hard to come by," Lepore writes. "Her obscurity is matched only by her brother's fame. If he meant to be Everyman, she is everyone else."

The unwritten stories of those left to obscurity for being disempowered, disenfranchised, for being quiet or unassuming or different, vociferously tell a story, too.

San Antonio celebrated its first Indigenous Peoples' Day on October 12, 2016, replacing the long-standing observance of Columbus Day on that date. In November 2015 the city council redesignated this day to honor contributions and sacrifices of the area's original inhabitants. Indigenous Peoples' Day recognizes Native people as the first inhabitants of the Americas, including the lands that later became the United States. It urges us to rethink history and points to the wide gaps there. The absence of the story becomes the story.

On June 18, 1954, six African American youths defied Jim Crow and dove into the Woodlawn Lake swimming pool. That night a cross—the calling card of the Ku Klux Klan—was burned in front of the pool. On June 19 the city council held an emergency meeting and voted to ban people of color from city swimming pools. Eventually a lawsuit was filed, and two years later the ordinance was repealed. This country was slow to acknowledge the courage of Rosa Parks, whose story we now share and celebrate. If only we could discover the names and stories of the six young men who went for that evening swim on that hot June day.

On October 30, 1912, a fire consumed Saint John's Orphanage and took the lives of three children and five nuns. The nuns risked their lives during the blaze to evacuate the children. When they heard the cries of a toddler still inside, Mother Mary of the Cross Rossiter ran inside to save the boy. They both perished.

In the foreword to *Black Ink*, Nikki Giovanni writes that her ancestors who came across the Atlantic on slave ships had no language to share with the slave owners. She imagines the moan of one suffering woman as a precursor to song: "The enslavers thought if we were not allowed to read and write, we would not appreciate who we were becoming, but they were wrong. We wrote sometimes with paper and we always wrote with song." She adds, "We write because we are lonely and scared and we need to keep our hearts open."

And that is the point. Benjamin Franklin was Jane's first teacher. From him she learned to write. It seems he gave her a great gift. The cruelty is that when he left, the lessons stopped. She was eleven. Though she saved his letters and they exist all these years later, the one-way correspondence resulting from the absence of her letters is, as Lepore describes it, "a house without windows, a left shoe, a pair of spectacles, smashed."

What were the names of the children at that San Antonio orphanage? Where did they come from? What were the turns of circumstance that brought them to share the spaces for the duration of their short lives with those nuns whose lives were given over in sacrifice for charism and charity? The laughter of the children at play, silenced then, remains a distinct part of history—as loud as a cry, as palpable and reassuring as the touch of a mother.

October 1, 1943

Police begin rounding up draft delinquents. A surprise dawn-to-dusk dragnet was sprung on vagrant men of military age. Police said the push had a twofold purpose of locating as many draft delinquents as possible and ridding the public places of idle men. Detectives were scattered all over the downtown area, including Maverick Park, the bandstand at Alamo Plaza, and Milam Square.

They were given instructions to question every loiterer or suspected loiterer thoroughly. By midnight more than one hundred men had been brought into the police station. Police captain Buck Haddox said that every draft delinquent located would be one less father who would have to be drafted. The drafting of fathers for the war effort began during the same week.

October 2, 1980

Police raid a North Side residence suspected of being a top-shelf brothel, arresting the alleged madam, Theresa Brown. They also confiscated a "trick list" of customers with more than three thousand names, including a number of local and state VIPs. A partial list was published in the local media. Police, acting under a court order, torched the confiscated list, but rumors persisted that Brown had a backup list. She later unsuccessfully ran for city council, challenging a councilmember who was rumored to have been one of her clients.

October 3, 1988

Texas Public Radio is on the air with KSTX 89.1 FM. For years news junkies had clamored for a local provider of National Public Radio, but funding construction of the station was almost out of reach. On the last day that the broadcasting license would permit, the station's transmitter was switched on. The new station was paired with

TPR reporter Joey Palacios interviews Mayor Ron Nirenberg, 2017

classical music station KPAC to form the nonprofit Texas Public Radio. Since first signing on, KSTX has been the San Antonio home of NPR's flagship news magazines. With listeners' support, KSTX added award-winning local newscasts, talk shows, and original programs.

October 4, 1873

After extensive renovations, San Fernando Cathedral is consecrated and reopened. The site for San Fernando church was selected on July 2, 1731, and was the center of life for the growing community. By 1840 the church had fallen into a state of disrepair. Half of its roof was gone and birds and bats made it their home. The original bell tower and part of the nave were razed. The new Gothic revival design included a gable roof, twin bell towers, and buttresses. The second tower would be completed in 1902.

October 5, 2015

The Mission Reach segment of the San Antonio River improvement project opens to the public. The plan was to take the concrete-channeled river south of downtown and restore it to its natural contours with a riparian woodland ecosystem of native plants. The eight-mile stretch provided a historic view of San Antonio that led up to the Spanish missions trail. The $271 million project was funded by the county, the city, the U.S. Army Corps of Engineers, and private donations from the San Antonio River Foundation.

October 6, 1968

HemisFair '68 comes to a close. The six-month run of the official World's Fair wrapped up with a visitor attendance total of 6,384,482. Themed the Confluence of Civilizations in the Americas, the fair paid tribute to the 250th anniversary of the city's founding in 1718. The sociopolitical turbulence of 1968 overshadowed the fair and may have reduced its overall success. Nevertheless it boosted the city's economy, recast the city's image, and left a legacy of downtown buildings and infrastructure to build a tourism economy. As the curtain came down on HemisFair, another rose for Fiestaland, which city officials planned as a permanent amusement park but which was an immediate flop.

October 7, 1992

The North American Free Trade Agreement is signed in the Alamo City. President George H. W. Bush, Canadian prime minister Brian Mulroney, and Mexican president Carlos Salinas de Gortari looked on as trade ministers from each respective country signed documents ending the negotiations for NAFTA. "This meeting marks a turning point in the history of our three countries," Bush told about two hundred dignitaries and business leaders packed into a courtyard at the Plaza Hotel. "We are creating the largest, richest, and most productive market in the entire world."

October 8, 1926

The Witte Museum opens—the longtime dream of Ellen Schulz Quillin, a botanist and high school teacher. Despite her dedication, the idea seemed out of reach until businessman Alfred W. Witte bequeathed $65,000 for a museum at Brackenridge Park. With additional funds from the city, the museum was built at the location of the original Spanish Acequia Madre. Quillin worked tirelessly through the late 1920s and 1930s to oversee construction, later managing the Witte in exchange for $1 a year.

October 9, 1860 〰〰〰〰〰〰〰〰〰〰〰〰〰〰〰〰〰〰〰〰〰〰〰

Governor Sam Houston speaks at San Pedro Springs Park. Despite being a slaveholder, he was hoping to persuade San Antonians to join him in opposing the Confederacy. In the two-hour speech, the leader of Texas independence and the former president of the Republic warned the throng of the deadly consequences of attempting to leave the Union. As he delivered the line "Political platforms will not stand," the wooden platform he was standing on collapsed. But the sixty-seven-year-old continued his speech.

October 10, 1973 〰〰〰〰〰〰〰〰〰〰〰〰〰〰〰〰〰〰〰〰〰〰

After being rented from Dallas, the Chaparrals, now the San Antonio Spurs, play their first American Basketball Association game. The matchup against the San Diego Conquistadors was played in front of six thousand new fans who rattled the rafters of HemisFair Arena. The roster featured George Karl and James Silas. George "the Iceman" Gervin joined the team soon after. The Spurs lost that game 121 to 106, but they would finish the first season with a 45-39 record. They were bought by a local ownership group and joined the National Basketball Association in 1976.

October 11, 1973

The U.S. Supreme Court hears the case *Espinoza v. Farah*, which asks if refusing to hire someone who is a legal resident alien but not a U.S. citizen is a violation of the 1964 Civil Rights Act. The act protects against discrimination based on national origin. Cecilia Espinoza, a San Antonio resident and citizen of Mexico, brought the case after she was refused employment by Farah Manufacturing because she was not a citizen. The Supreme Court ruled eight to one in favor of Farah, holding that employment discrimination against noncitizens is allowed even if they have legal work status.

October 12, 2016

The city has its first official Indigenous Peoples' Day, on the date traditionally set aside to celebrate Italian explorer Christopher Columbus, credited with discovering the New World. In November 2015 the city council designated the day to honor the contributions and sacrifices of the original inhabitants of the San Antonio area. A growing number of cities and states recognize October 12 as Indigenous Peoples' Day, but Texas does not.

October 13, 1897

Officials announce that there is no yellow fever in San Antonio. Nonetheless the city was in a panic, so much so that the International–Great Northern Railroad added passenger rail cars to accommodate the many people fleeing town. No one wanted a repeat of the yellow fever epidemic of 1867 that devastated South Texas and coastal communities; approximately four thousand Texans died and close to forty thousand were infected. The disease dramatically changed San Antonio and the other parts of the state. In 1897 San Antonio officials acted quickly to reassure the public, surrounding communities, and railroad officials that there was no public health crisis and that no quarantine of the city was necessary. The yellow fever panic was triggered when a local man fell ill. His malady, however, turned out to be malaria.

October 14, 1967 ///

County commissioner Albert Peña Jr. calls the lack of a free hot lunch program in the San Antonio Independent School District a disgrace. Peña was the first Mexican American elected to the Commissioners Court in 1956. He served there until 1972 and frequently used the post to fight against segregation, issues of poverty, and other injustices across South Texas. He was a founder of the Mexican American Unity Council and the Mexican American Legal Defense and Educational Fund. "Included in the school district are some of the worst slums in the United States. The result of high unemployment, low wages, and job discrimination," he said. "Many of

these children go to school hungry every day. Too many
do not go to school for that same reason."

October 15, 1866 〰〰〰〰〰〰〰〰〰〰〰〰〰〰〰〰〰〰〰〰

A new footbridge over the San Antonio River is opened
as part of a major improvement project to widen Commerce Street. The crossing is at the site of the historic
main ford and has long been a focal point for the city. An
iron truss bridge was built in 1880 and replaced by the
present concrete bridge in 1915. The south side of the
bridge contains a sculpture of an Indian man, *The First
Inhabitant*, whose hands once held a drinking fountain.

October 16, 2003 〰〰〰〰〰〰〰〰〰〰〰〰〰〰〰〰〰〰〰〰〰

Ground is broken for the Toyota truck manufacturing
plant in south San Antonio. Local leaders said bringing
Toyota would be the single biggest economic issue the
city had ever undertaken. The first Tundra truck rolled off
the assembly line on November 17, 2006. Toyota's arrival
changed the economic picture for the city, which had
been losing manufacturing jobs and witnessed a string
of factory closures.

October 17, 1909 〰〰〰〰〰〰〰〰〰〰〰〰〰〰〰〰〰〰〰〰〰

President William Howard Taft arrives in the city to
lay the cornerstone for a new chapel at Fort Sam

Gift Chapel, Fort Sam Houston

Houston. The Gift Chapel was quite literally a gift from the people of San Antonio to the army post. Taft was on a coast-to-coast train tour in a specially built rail car for the thirteen-thousand-mile journey. The previous day he had been in El Paso, where he shook hands with Porfirio Díaz, the president of Mexico, and discussed improving trade relations.

October 18, 1835

The Mexican commandant of San Antonio, Martín Perfecto de Cos, rejects a truce offer from Stephen F. Austin. General Cos, in Texas to end the rebellion, told Austin he could not enter into negotiations because he refused to acknowledge the Army of Texas. He also called Austin an ignorant traitor who would lead his people into a disastrous war. On December 11, during the Siege of Béxar, Cos and his garrison took a defensive position inside the Alamo mission. They were outmatched by the Texicans and surrendered. Cos was defeated and returned to Mexico.

October 19, 1919

The League of Women Voters of Texas is formed in San Antonio. The nonpartisan political organization was created after a woman's right to vote was recognized in Texas, a year before the right was recognized nationally with the 1920 ratification of the Nineteenth Amendment. The league's mission was to educate all voters of their rights and of the issues and candidates on the ballot. The newly enfranchised women decided they would dissolve the Texas Equal Suffrage Association and reorganize as the Texas League of Women Voters.

October 20, 1961

The McFarlin diamond is donated to the Witte Museum. The 49.73 carat emerald-cut canary diamond, once the property of an Indian maharajah, was set in a necklace with an 18-karat gold mounting surrounded by emeralds. The diamond was housed in a special room in the museum until it was stolen in broad daylight on June 14, 1968. At the time the diamond was valued at $365,000. The thief smashed through the "shatter-proof" glass display case, left the hammer behind, and placed a folding lawn chair in the room's doorway to prevent an alarm-triggered security gate from lowering and trapping him. Witnesses told police he walked briskly through the museum and ran to a waiting car. Roadblocks were set up across the city, but the raider and the diamond got away. The thief was eventually apprehended and confessed to the crime, but the diamond has never been recovered.

October 21, 1954

San Antonio gets its third mayor for 1954. The political musical chairs at city hall settle with R. N. White Sr. as mayor. He had been appointed to the city council that day to replace his son R. N. "Dick" White Jr., who resigned rather than face a recall election. Moments after the elder White was appointed, he was nominated and elected to the mayor's office by a coalition of councilmembers who themselves had also been recently appointed after recall-related mass resignations. White served as mayor for almost six months. City elections were held on April 5,

1955, with the Good Government League ticket riding a landslide into city hall.

October 22, 1861

A Confederate invasion of the Western Territory marches from San Antonio. Known as the New Mexico Campaign, 3,200 men were led by Henry Hopkins Sibley with the mission to conquer and occupy the West all the way to San Diego Bay. Sibley raised three regiments in San Antonio—the Fourth, Fifth, and Seventh Texas Mounted Volunteers. He underestimated opposition to the Confederates in the West, however, and the invasion was an unmitigated disaster. Only half of the brigade made it back to San Antonio, having failed at all of their goals.

October 23, 1960

San Antonio is gaga for John Wayne and his movie *The Alamo*, staging a three-day celebration for the Duke, including a twenty-thousand-person square dance and a thirty-foot cake in the shape of the Alamo that Wayne carved up with a bowie knife, all leading to the film's world premiere at the Woodlawn Theatre. The epic was Wayne's personal dream and ambition. He was the producer and director and starred in the role of Davy Crockett. He said he wanted the movie to inspire Americans during the Cold War era.

Alamo movie poster, 1960

October 24, 1942

San Antonio buys the San Antonio Public Service Company, known today as CPS Energy, in a $34 million no-cash deal. The electric utility ran the electric power plants, gas lines, and streetcars and was owned by the American Light and Traction Company, which was forced to sell because of federal antitrust laws. The purchase was controversial. Doubters said city hall had no business owning a utility, and the city government's history of corruption made many question whether it could be trusted to run the electric utility. But seventy-six years later CPS Energy has generated more than $7 billion for the city and is a national leader in energy production.

October 25, 1938

An election is held to improve the San Antonio River. The election would allow the sale of $75,000 in bonds matched with $325,000 in federal funds. Plaza Hotel manager Jack White pushed for the plan, which passed seventy-four to two. Coincidentally seventy-one of the voters lived in White's hotel. Project engineer E. P. Arneson said the improvements would include an outdoor performing theater with walks built along the riverbanks and promised that when complete the river would be as useful as a street.

October 26, 1955 〰〰〰〰〰〰〰〰〰〰〰〰〰〰〰〰〰〰〰〰〰〰〰〰〰〰

The Supreme Court of Texas clears the way for San Antonio to participate in the Canyon Dam project. After major floods on the Guadalupe River in 1936 and 1938, state leaders pressured the federal government to help control river flooding. Meanwhile, during the drought San Antonio watched its aquifer wells drop to historic low levels. On August 17, 1956, the J-17 index well recorded its lowest point. City leaders saw the developing project as a needed water lifeline. The San Antonio Water Board wanted 100,000 acre-feet of water per year from the lake, but a state law prohibited transfer of water from one watershed to another, and the Guadalupe-Blanco River Authority protested, saying the Guadalupe Valley needed "every drop" of water for its own development and San Antonio needed to develop its own supply. The court victory didn't settle the controversy. On July 5, 1957, the Texas Water Board turned down San Antonio's application and doomed its water diversion dream. Construction of Canyon Dam was started on June 27, 1958.

October 27, 1940 〰〰〰〰〰〰〰〰〰〰〰〰〰〰〰〰〰〰〰〰〰〰〰〰〰〰

Novelist H. G. Wells is in San Antonio to address the United States Brewers' Association. By chance, radio dramatist and actor Orson Welles was also there to speak at the San Pedro Playhouse en route to Tucson. It was two years after the panic-causing "War of the Worlds" radio broadcast, adapted from the Wells novel, and the two discussed the public's reaction to the Martian invasion. But there was another world at war on the two luminaries' minds. H. G. Wells warned about the war in Europe with Nazi Germany and said Americans were fortunate that "you haven't got the war right under your chins."

October 28, 1835

In the opening engagement of the Siege of Béxar, the Battle of Concepción takes place on the grounds of Mission Concepción. Texican troops under Stephen F. Austin were engaged by Mexican troops commanded by Col. Domingo Ugartechea. The thirty-minute battle resulted in seventy-five Mexican troops killed. Richard Andrews was the only Texican casualty. The next day the Mexican army fled to San Antonio, where the Texans dared not chase them. The victory seemed to confirm what was suspected about the Mexican soldiers—that they were poorly armed and trained and didn't really want to be fighting in Texas. The Texans were proving to be highly motivated and well-armed, with solid leadership. The battle also proved to the world that the Texans were serious about their independence.

October 29, 1933

Stating that the International Walkathon Marathon violates an ordinance against public exhibitions, city officials try to shut it down by cutting off electricity to the Walk-athon Stadium at Augusta and Navarro Streets. The endurance contest began on October 3 with twenty-seven couples committing to continual movement around the clock except for a fifteen-minute break every hour. As the couples marched, walked, danced, and sang, the conflict with city hall was dragged into court, which refused to step in. The walkathon continued until November 13. The winning couple, Joe Landiso and Vina Walker, hoofed it for 972 hours and were awarded $250 each.

October 30, 1912

A tragic fire consumes Saint John's Orphanage and takes the lives of three children and five nuns. The orphanage was founded in 1869 when three Sisters of Charity of the Incarnate Word welcomed and cared for abandoned and orphaned children. In 1912 it was home to eighty-seven boys and eight nuns who cared for them. The blaze ignited at about 4:30 a.m. and quickly spread through the building. The nuns worked to evacuate the children's dormitory, but while in the yard they heard the cries of a toddler still inside. Mother Mary of the Cross Rossiter ran into the burning building to save the boy and became trapped. They both perished in the fire. The orphanage was eventually rebuilt and renamed Saint Peter–Saint Joseph's Children's Home.

October 31, 1967 ///

In one of the biggest scares in the city's history some of the lifting rods snap and almost send HemisFair Tower's top house crashing to the ground. The cupcake-shaped structure was built on the ground and hoisted 579 feet into position. The next few days were critical. Engineers needed to secure the top house in place and find a way to resume lifting it. Construction cranes from around the state were scrounged, and the job was completed in time for the fair's opening six months later.

When designer Kate Spade and travel documentarian Anthony Bourdain died within weeks of each other in summer 2018, both from suicide, pundits and armchair analysts offered flimsy conjectures as to why. But who can really say what happens in the mind of someone who is hurting? When the news cycle lands on the passing of someone who made us laugh, someone whose intelligence and talents we admire, we can't imagine their motives.

Carol Burnett was born in San Antonio. Both of her parents were alcoholics, and she was raised by her grandmother in Hollywood. Burnett has spoken often of how difficult life was and said going to the movies several times a week with her grandmother influenced her career as an entertainer. Burnett's daughter Carrie battled substance abuse as a teenager. She died in 2002 at age thirty-eight from pneumonia, a complication that resulted from treatment for lung and brain cancer. Burnett continues to entertain her legions of fans in TV appearances and is the benefactor of scholarships at the University of California at Los Angeles and the University of Hawaii.

Imitation is the highest form of flattery, they say. On her wildly popular and long-running CBS variety show on Saturday nights, Burnett put on memorable skits spoofing the black-and-white movies she enjoyed with her grandmother. One actress she frequently imitated with Groucho Marx brows and a sullen, jowly scowl was Lucille Fay LeSueur, also known as Joan Crawford. After Crawford's birth in San Antonio, her father deserted the family. Other hardships brought about by poverty followed before she would make her way to Hollywood and her storied life as a movie star and diva.

Another star of the screen and Texas native, Audie Murphy, was one of the most decorated combat soldiers of World War II, earning every possible combat award for valor from the U.S. Army. Murphy's father abandoned the family when he was young, and his mother died when he was a teenager. He dropped out of school in the fifth grade to pick cotton.

After the war Murphy became a Hollywood star, raised quarter horses, and was an accomplished songwriter of some note. He also suffered from what today would be diagnosed as post-traumatic stress disorder, and it has been widely reported that he slept with a loaded handgun under his pillow and was addicted to sleeping pills. He spoke often about his problems with PTSD, what was referred to in those days as battle fatigue or shell shock. He was having financial problems right up until his untimely death at age forty-five in a plane crash in Virginia in 1971. He was interred with full military honors at Arlington National Cemetery.

As a result of legislation introduced by the U.S. congressman Olin Teague five months after Murphy's death, the Audie L. Murphy Memorial VA Hospital was dedicated. In 1973 it was established as part of the South Texas Veterans Health Care System in San Antonio.

The band R.E.M. filmed the video for the song "Everybody Hurts" in November 1992 on I-10 between Fredericksburg Road and Colorado Street. Audiences have perceived an anti-suicide message in the tune and adopted it as a mental health anthem. Drummer Bill Berry, who penned the song, said it was meant to connect to those who feel no hope. Singer Michael Stipe said the song "instantly belonged to everyone except us, and that honestly means the world to me."

Most assume that R.E.M. stands for "rapid eye movement," but over time the name's origins have become less enigmatic. In a 2007 speech delivered when the band was inducted into the Rock and Roll Hall of Fame, Stipe noted that his grandmother said the acronym stands for "remember every moment." The words seem to be a salve rather than an imperative. Remember the good times too, not just those things that bring us to despair.

Carol Burnett's childhood home was moved a few blocks from its original location on West Commerce Street. Today it is a literacy center for underprivileged children, founded by Henry and Mary Alice Cisneros. Returning to that childhood home in November 2018, Burnett recalled roller skating on the uneven sidewalk and falling and hurting her knee. Assessing the situation, she donned her skates inside the house, where she could roll along on a smooth and even path.

November 1, 1992

San Antonio's telephone area code changes to 210 from 512, which formerly covered Austin and central Texas. Southwestern Bell officials said the growth in San Antonio's population and telecommunications services had depleted available phone numbers. One explanation for why Austin was allowed to keep the 512 code is that it would be too expensive for state offices to change. In 2016 the creation of the 726 area code required residents to dial a ten-digit number when making a local phone call.

November 2, 1887

The *Daily Light* mentions that on this All Saints Day a number of people are decorating the graves of deceased friends. There is a brief note in the paper again, on November 2, 1892, about the city's celebration of All Saints Day and All Souls Day: "The decorations of the graves at the Mexican cemetery were many and beautiful." Newspaper staff were unable to recognize the observance Día de los Muertos, or the Day of the Dead, which dates back three thousand years in the Americas. With the arrival of the missionaries, it blended the Feast Day of All Souls with colonial Catholic teachings.

Día de los Muertos

November 3, 1944

New Orleans–born trumpet player Don Albert opens the
Keyhole Club at 728 Iowa Street. Some of the era's greatest entertainers performed at the Chitlin' Circuit nightclub, including Duke Ellington, Sarah Vaughan, and Louis
Armstrong. The Keyhole, which closed and reopened in
1950 at 1618 Poplar Street, welcomed all races, and this
attracted the attention of police commissioner George

M. Roper. After winning a May 22, 1951, runoff election where he was the only name on the ballot, Roper, a vocal segregationist, launched a crusade to wipe out vice and fight integration in San Antonio. On June 22 Roper declared that the Keyhole's roof was unsafe and ordered the establishment closed. Albert took the city to court, and on October 17 the Fourth Court of Appeals ruled in favor of the club. The ruling blasted Roper for "self-made, self-tried, and self-executed law—the excessive use of authority." This was seen as an early civil rights victory and a blow against segregation in San Antonio.

November 4, 1994

The San Antonio Spurs are set to play their home opener game at the Alamodome, but during the fanfare of pre-game introductions an indoor firework display triggers sensors for a high-pressure water cannon. For more than three minutes some twelve thousand gallons of water rained down on the crowd and court. Hundreds of fans were soaked, and the game was delayed for fifty minutes. The Spurs lost 123 to 118 to the Golden State Warriors.

November 5, 1990

Ground is broken for the Alamodome. The city moved forward with construction despite ongoing legal and personality clashes over the multipurpose facility's proposed name. After the city announced the name, it came to light that it was trademarked by another company. The city then floated other names to little enthusiasm, including the Fiesta Dome and the MegaDome. A deal was eventually struck to purchase the Alamodome name. The facility, however, is not a true architectural dome.

November 6, 1931 //

Congressman Harry Wurzbach dies in office. Representing the fourteenth district based in Seguin, Wurzbach was the only Republican congressman from Texas. His sudden death created a political earthquake in Washington, D.C. A special election held in San Antonio was won by Democrat Richard M. Kleberg, which gave the Democrats a one-seat majority and control of the U.S. House, which they held for all but four of the next sixty-three years. Kleberg, heir to the King Ranch in South Texas, was not keen on the daily duties of being a congressman, so he delegated much of the job to his congressional secretary, Lyndon Johnson.

November 7, 1835 //

The Declaration of November 7, 1835, is adopted by the Consultation at San Felipe. The document was a declaration of causes for Texas to take up arms against Mexico. The rebellion had already begun, and Mexican troops were marching against San Antonio. The justification provided was not secession but Mexico's abandonment of its constitution of 1824. It's not clear whether this argument was sincere or a strategic bid to win support from factions in Mexico and native Tejanos against the dictator general Santa Anna.

November 8, 1977 〰〰〰〰〰〰〰〰〰〰〰〰〰〰〰〰〰〰〰〰〰〰〰〰〰〰〰

Area voters approve the creation of the Metropolitan Transit Authority by a margin of nearly two to one. The authority was given access to a one-half-cent sales tax by San Antonio and seven other incorporated municipalities. The authority, which became known as VIA, purchased the San Antonio Transit System assets and began operations on March 1, 1978. The drive to pass the initiative was led by Mayor Lila Cockrell and Councilman Henry Cisneros, who bucked conventional wisdom that predicted rejection at the polls. They both said the city's future depended on a modern bus system. Opponents were divided; some didn't want the city council to have control of public transit, and others wanted no tax increase or public dollars funding the buses. San Antonio was the first city in the state to approve a transit authority and the first in the nation to pass it on the first try. On November 2, 2004, voters approved the formation of the Advanced Transportation District, which uses a quarter-cent sales tax to fund transportation improvement projects carried out by VIA, the city, and the Texas Department of Transportation.

November 9, 1935

The Texas Rangers and a Texas Department of Safety squad raid the Turf Bar on Soledad Street, the Mansion Nightclub on Burr Road, and Riverside Gardens on Houston Street. The three illegal gambling houses operated in the open undisturbed by law enforcement. The raids came as a surprise to county sheriff Albert W. West, who told a reporter, "I didn't even know they were in town." Among the equipment seized were dice tables, roulette wheels, blackjack tables, poker chips, and slot machines. Inspector Lee Miller said the raid was planned in Austin with the assignment "to clean up San Antonio. I've been in other Texas cities and this is the most wide open. It's like Monte Carlo." Miller said they also planned to raid the Shadowland nightclub on Blanco Road and the Olmos Night Club, but word had already spread that the heat was on.

November 10, 1891

The Fashion Theater fire engulfs the west block of Military Plaza. The four-hour fire broke out that evening in the theater's property room when an oil-burning lamp flared and exploded. The fire quickly consumed the theater's backhouse. Horse-pulled fire brigade wagons soon arrived, but the flames were already piercing the second-story windows and licking the building's dome. Barrels of whiskey stored in the cellar exploded, and the fire spread to the entire block. A number of businesses were gutted, including a hide and pelt trader, a printing office, the Italian Society meeting room, a laundry, and a barbershop. Earlier that year, to some controversy, the city had dismissed its volunteer firefighting outfits to create its first paid fire department. While professional firefighters fought the blaze, the old volunteers turned out to heckle them. Despite these difficulties the firefighters contained the blaze and saved the Spanish Governor's Palace.

November 11, 1940 〰〰〰〰〰〰〰〰〰〰〰〰〰〰〰〰〰〰

There is a minute of silence, the playing of taps, an Armistice Day parade, and the dedication of the

Alamo cenotaph, 2005

Alamo cenotaph, *Spirit of Sacrifice,* in Alamo Plaza near the entrance to the Alamo. Several locations for the cenotaph were proposed, including Travis Park and in front of the Menger Hotel. The location had no historic significance, and it was not built on the spot where the funeral pyres burned the bodies of fallen Texas heroes. The monument was designed by San Antonio architecture firm Adams and Adams, and its sculptural parts were conceived and executed by Italian-born sculptor Pompeo Coppini. Begun in 1937, the cenotaph took two years to complete.

November 12, 1914

Otto Koehler is fatally shot by one of his mistresses. Koehler was the president of the San Antonio Brewing Association, which produced Pearl Beer. His invalid wife and his two German mistresses were all named Emma. He was distraught when one of his lovers, Emma Dumpke, eloped and moved to Saint Louis. Koehler then turned his full attention to Emma Burgemeister, nicknamed Hedda, but that affair soured and she allegedly shot him. Burgemeister was indicted for the killing, but when the case was called for trial, she fled back to Europe to nurse the war wounded. Eventually she returned and was put on trial. She was found not guilty and married one of the jurors. Koehler's wife Emma took over the brewery and ran the business with spectacular success.

November 13, 1917

Sidney Johnson Brooks Jr. dies in his final training flight at Kelly Field when his Curtiss JN-4 nosedives into the ground. The twenty-two-year-old Brooks, who was training for a commission as a military aviator, was the son of a local judge and had worked as a reporter for the *San Antonio Light*. He was a law student at the University of Texas when he answered the call for the American Flying Corps. Brooks was awarded his wings and commission posthumously, and Brooks Air Force Base was named in his honor.

November 14, 1964

The Brackenridge Park sky ride takes to the air. The attraction was the vision of Randall Clay, president of the Aerial Transportation Company. The idea was pitched to the city council as a ride that would stretch twelve hundred feet and cost fifty cents for a roundtrip ticket. The council approved the idea on condition that the city would receive a quarter of the profits. The tramway stood a hundred feet tall and stretched from the zoo entrance to the top of Gorilla Hill at the Japanese Tea Gardens. The sky ride ended its run in 1999.

November 15, 1976

Ramsey Muñiz, a two-time-unsuccessful Raza Unida candidate for Texas governor, is indicted in San Antonio.

Muñiz was accused of smuggling marijuana into the United States from Mexico. It was the second time in nearly four months that Muñiz had been indicted for drug smuggling. A Corpus Christi attorney, he ran for governor in 1972 and 1974 and lost both times to Dolph Briscoe. Later Muñiz pleaded guilty to one count and served five years in prison. In 1994 he was arrested with ninety pounds of cocaine and was given a life sentence. With failing health he was released in 2018. Muñiz claims he was a political prisoner who was incarcerated due to his outspoken activism for Mexican Americans.

November 16, 1926

The Nix Professional Building, promoted as the first "medical mall" in the world, opens with great fanfare. The Gothic-style, twenty-three-story building was conceived by Joseph M. Nix to house not only a hospital but also doctors' offices, medical support facilities, and a parking garage. Among the notables born at the Nix are comedian Carol Burnett, former HUD secretary Henry Cisneros, and Iran-Contra conspirator Oliver North.

November 17, 1934

Lyndon B. Johnson marries Claudia Alta "Lady Bird" Taylor at Saint Mark's Episcopal Church. Johnson didn't have a wedding band for his bride and asked his friend Dan Quill, postmaster of San Antonio, to get one. Quill bought a wedding band at the nearby Sears, located in what is now the Tower Life Building, for $2.50. After the wedding the couple had dinner at the Saint Anthony Hotel and spent their wedding night at the Plaza Hotel.

November 18, 1948 〰〰〰〰〰〰〰〰〰〰〰〰〰〰〰〰〰

The city council passes a resolution cutting off the utilities for the newest city in Bexar County. On November 13 residents of Balcones Heights voted thirty-five to three to incorporate. News that the two-and-a-half-mile area would not be part of San Antonio angered Mayor Alfred Callaghan, who said he did not want to nurture another municipality on city's border that could enjoy all the city's conveniences without paying for them. He ordered the termination of electric power, water service, garbage pickup, and police and fire protection.

November 19, 1910 〰〰〰〰〰〰〰〰〰〰〰〰〰〰〰〰〰

"There is absolutely no danger of a general revolution in Mexico," Albino R. Nuncio declares at the International Fair in San Antonio. The Mexican envoy admitted that in every representative government there are parties opposed to the ruling government, but "the men antagonistic to President Porfirio Díaz are in the small minority." Two days earlier Francisco Madero had left San Antonio, where he had been in exile, to return to Mexico, accompanied by his brothers. He told supporters he was going on a hunting trip, but he was on his way to direct the operations of the revolutionists in Mexico. While in San Antonio, Madero had called for the revolution to begin at 6 p.m. on November 20. Following the resignation of Díaz on May 25, 1911, Madero became president of Mexico.

November 20, 1909

The Gunter Hotel opens. The edifice was erected on the site of the Mahncke Hotel, which before that was the Vance House. A hotel or inn has been on the site since 1837. Previously it was the location of army barracks used by Robert E. Lee and the Confederate army during the Civil War. The eight-story, 301-room hotel was built by the San Antonio Hotel Company and named for Jot Gunter, a rancher and real estate developer who was one of the major investors. The Panic of 1907 delayed the construction. It was the largest building in San Antonio at the time and deemed a skyscraper by the local press.

November 21, 1992

The band R.E.M. shoots the music video "Everybody Hurts" on I-10 between Fredericksburg Road and Colorado Street. A handful of San Antonians were hired as extras for the video, which shows people stuck in a traffic jam with their inner monologues appearing as subtitles. Hal McCloskey, who was spotted selling flowers on the River Walk, was cast as a man ripping pages from a Bible and tossing them down into the traffic jam. The song has become an anti-suicide anthem.

November 22, 1963

Catholic churches and other houses of worship across the city overflow as news spreads of the assassination of President John F. Kennedy, who was in San Antonio with First Lady Jacqueline Kennedy the day before. More than a hundred thousand jubilant San Antonians had lined the twenty-six-mile parade route as the presidential motorcade passed. Kennedy had been so moved by the enthusiasm that he vowed to return. Twenty-four hours later the scene along the same route was one of people overcome with grief.

November 23, 2018

The Texas Court of Criminal Appeals exonerates the "San Antonio Four," who were wrongfully convicted and imprisoned in 1994 for the alleged sexual assault of two young girls. Cleared of the convictions were Elizabeth Ramirez, Cassandra Rivera, Kristie Mayhugh, and Anna Vasquez. They had proclaimed their innocence throughout the years. The charges were prompted by accusations from two of Ramirez's nieces, ages seven and nine, who testified that the four women sexually assaulted them during a weekend visit with their aunt. Over time the damning testimony began to unravel. In 2012 the younger accuser recanted and said she had been pressured to lie. Vasquez was released from prison on parole in 2012 after serving twelve years, and the other three were released on bond in 2013 pending appeals.

November 24, 1993 //

The city council gives the farmers' market a new name, Market Square, along with a new plan. As San Antonio became settled and urbanized, the land, which the king of Spain had gifted to the community in 1730, became known as the Hay Market and then in 1899 as the Market House, with a grand building and plaza designed by Alfred Giles. In 1938 the Works Progress Administration replaced the building with the Municipal Truck Market, but with the advent of the modern grocery store the last produce was sold there in 1975. Market Square was renovated into an enclosed, air-conditioned *mercado* on the western end of downtown and became a popular tourist shopping area and a public space to keep local culture alive.

November 25, 1931 //

The U.S. Treasury Department orders San Antonio's U.S. collector of customs to lift a 9 p.m. curfew on the U.S.-Mexico international bridges in Laredo, Del Rio, Eagle Pass, and Zapata. Under the new order they would operate until midnight. The action came after pleas and petitions from border city mayors and county judges stating that longer operating hours would facilitate greater trade and commerce with Mexico. The bridges had previously operated all night, but a complaint from congressmen said conditions in Mexico were leading to business and moral corruption in the United States.

November 26, 1835

The Grass Fight takes place—the last engagement in the siege of San Antonio before the final Texan assault on the town. That morning Erastus "Deaf" Smith rode into the Texas camp with the news that the Mexican cavalry was approaching San Antonio. Thinking the column was carrying silver to purchase supplies and pay the Mexican army, Jim Bowie attacked at a ravine near the Alazán Creek. The Texans defeated the Mexican forces and captured the pack animals only to discover their prize was grass carried to feed the army animals.

November 27, 1980

The first official Raul Jimenez Thanksgiving Dinner is served to the San Antonio community. Known for his magnetic personality, Jimenez was an entrepreneur in the food industry. In 1979 he personally funded and served a Thanksgiving meal for five thousand seniors. Seeing a greater need, the following year he opened the event to the community and a local tradition was born. In 1980 six thousand attendees received turkey and all the trimmings. In 2018 more than twenty-five thousand guests were served and entertained.

November 28, 1975 〰〰〰〰〰〰〰〰〰〰〰〰〰〰〰〰

The city's first holiday lighting ceremony takes place on the River Walk. The idea was conceived by "Bill" McCormick, president of Joske's and a member of a downtown merchants' association. McCormick, who was concerned about the trend of holiday shoppers skipping downtown and going to malls, suggested a spectacular show on the first Friday after Thanksgiving to dazzle the consumers back. He sold others on the plan to spend about $25,000 to string thirty-five thousand white decorative lights along the river bend.

November 29, 1963 〰〰〰〰〰〰〰〰〰〰〰〰〰〰〰〰〰〰〰

The Lee Volunteers face the Brackenridge Eagles at Alamo Stadium in what some have called the greatest Texas high school football game ever played. There were seventeen kickoffs, no punts, and only three penalties. Lee had ten wins and no losses. Brackenridge had an 8-2 record and was the defending state champion. Lee won the game 55-48. The game was played against the backdrop of the Kennedy assassination, which had occurred a week earlier. Lee's Linus Baer went on to play for the Longhorns at the University of Texas. Brackenridge player Warren McVea played for the Kansas City Chiefs and won a Super Bowl.

The Argyle

November 30, 1860 ~~~~~~

Attorney and rancher Charles Anderson delivers a fiery abolitionist speech in Alamo Plaza. Anderson's ranch covered what is now Alamo Heights; his ranch house is now the Argyle. His pro-Union speech stirred up an angry mob, and the Golden Circle, a secret society that supported secession, arrested him. He managed to escape to Mexico with his family and sold his San Antonio land. After President Lincoln sent him on a pro-Union speaking tour of Europe, Anderson joined the Union army and later served as governor of Ohio and Kentucky. The Argyle is now a private club that supports the Texas Biomedical Research Institute.

DECEMBER

n the essay "¡Que Vivan los Colores!" in *A House of My Own*, Sandra Cisneros, author and MacArthur Foundation grant winner, describes the collective hysteria that occurred in 1997 when she painted her house a shade of periwinkle. She recalls that many wrote to her in support—men from jail cells, children in schools, and even someone claiming to be the great-grand-descendant of Davy Crockett. The parry-and-dodge of the letters to the editor and water cooler conversations underscored the idea that change in a city is relative.

On April 7, 1966, the Toudouze family was forced to evacuate their home at 123 Wyoming Street to make way for HemisFair. As bulldozers prepared to demolish the house, Frank Toudouze played "May the Good Lord Bless and Keep You" on his harmonica. His seventy-five-year-old mother wept as sheriff deputies broke the door locks to evict the family. Toudouze insisted that the process by which the city took possession of the property was not legal and that his neighborhood was not a "slum area." Folks still rally around the Toudouze family when they hear the story, even as they admire the skyline, which shows unmistakable symbols of change stretching upward.

Plato has long been credited with saying that "any city, however small, is in fact divided into two, one the city of the poor, the other of the rich; these are at war with one another." In literature the freeway, generally built through a city's more economically depressed areas, symbolizes both destruction and progress. Patricia Preciado Martin writes, in "The Journey," that "the Freeway has cut the rivers from the people. The Freeway blocks the sunshine. The drone of the traffic buzzes like a giant unsleeping bee, a new music in the barrio." And yet we all know what an important and integral part of modern life the freeway is, representing travel, growth, and progress.

Ernst Jünger wrote: "One need merely visit the marketplace and the graveyard to determine whether a city is in both physical and metaphysical order." Many San Antonians understand the uncomfortable truth of this statement and can name plenty of other ways division and disparity have been sown over centuries.

Other things have brought the city together, too. In 2013 eleven-year-old Sebastien De La Cruz sang the national anthem during the third game of the NBA finals, dressed in a traditional mariachi outfit honoring his Mexican heritage and that of a great majority of the population of San Antonio. He promptly became the target of cyberbullying and trolling. The slurs and racist attacks aimed at a Mexican American boy singing the national anthem of the United States are confounding.

Some in the city rallied around the young man, but it was Sebastien De La Cruz who represented us all in the best way possible, with poise and dignity. "With the racism remarks, to be honest, it's just the people how they were raised," he said. "My father and my mother told me that you should never judge people by how they look."

Maybe San Antonio Spurs coach Gregg Popovich took a tip from De La Cruz in recent years, as he has been vocal in defending multiple disenfranchised groups. The Spurs also seem to encourage unity in a city that is not always united, not always served equally. That's the way it seems to be in large cities with winning sports teams, but San Antonio reached a kind of big-city, big-league status thanks in large part to the several winning seasons and multiple championship wins of the late nineties and early aughts.

"The first requisite to happiness is that a man be born in a famous city," according to Euripides. Perhaps it is more the case that a famous city requires happy citizens, for, as Shakespeare wrote, "What is a city but the people?" When one reviews the pages of a city's history, the only things we see are people, protagonists in a drama with multiple conflicts. The essence of any story is its conflict, which is essentially a problem with loss. The character has lost something, is looking for something. The character feels a void, some loss, but doesn't know what it is, and that seems to be the problem. In writing classes, we're told to write "from the wound." We read from wounds, too. We write and read to know ourselves and each other better.

If we are asked to vacate our home in the name of progress, progress becomes a wound. If we stand in support of our nation by singing its most sacred song and are summarily heckled or worse, we understand patriotism from that wound.

When Yolanda Saldívar gunned down Selena Quintanilla-Pérez on March 31, 1995, the world lost what it could have known about the next big crossover star. Many of us in San Antonio understand the silenced potential—but also her unmistakable charisma and talent from her death—from that wound.

There are many strange mythologies connected with San Antonio, among them the story of the haunted railroad tracks and the ghost children who can execute the herculean feat of pushing a car out of the way of a train barreling toward it. It is one of the well-worn chapters in the story of a haunted San Antonio. Some accounts connect the tale to a 1938 accident involving the deaths of thirty children. All of the stories told from all of those wounds speak of a pain so magnified that it could only be conceived of in this way that somehow brings the children back to life.

History is full of such improvisations, such hyperbole and distortions. Some of these emerge as a result of an inability to reckon with the truth and a failure to understand the past.

Native peoples were guided by a spirituality that extended to all animals. They hunted for food, first asking permission of the animal's spirit. For example, there was an honoring of a deer that provided life and nourishment. The sacrifice was necessary and unavoidable, but the hunter acknowledged the fallen in order to assign it dignity.

Among the hunter-gatherers, the land was owned in common; the concept of land as private property did not exist the way we understand it in a city governed by zoning and ordinances and laws. The idea of selling and buying land was unheard-of, and the people felt a profound disdain for the idea of those negotiations.

That the Toudouze family was evicted, their home razed, and life as they knew it changed forever would be an even more profound loss had the story not been shared. For in the retelling we could somehow, in the ways of the Native peoples, acknowledge the sacrifice and assign the family their rightful dignity.

The truth of stories is based on perspective, and this is how we consider history. We don't get to time travel and observe the past or get into the minds of those who were there. But that doesn't mean we shouldn't keep our eyes wide open. We should read widely and deeply and make sense of what has happened and what continues to happen all around us, even what seems incredible and insurmountable today. We can never see or experience firsthand the stories passed down through our long history as a city, but they can still show us where to look, what to focus on, how to represent them as citizens who have suffered losses, been changed for good or ill, and learned about ourselves and each other, as we keep moving into the future.

December 1, 1932 〰〰〰〰〰〰〰〰〰〰〰〰〰〰〰〰〰〰〰〰〰

The San Antonio Public Service Company tells the city council it will abolish the streetcar system in favor of motorized buses, claiming the move will modernize the city's transportation system. In 1926 the streetcar system had reached its peak with ninety miles of track. Then the Depression's economic brakes curbed ticket demand. It didn't help that the trolleys were rundown, slow, and exposed to the weather and didn't serve the new communities that were developed farther away from the city center. Citizens objected to the loss of the streetcars and argued that it would be a step backward for the city. The city's first mule-pulled trolleys were seen in 1875 walking from downtown to San Pedro Springs. Electric trolleys were introduced in 1890, with three trolley companies competing. In 1898 the San Antonio Traction Company bought out the rail rivals and introduced uniform fares and line-to-line transfers, and in 1918 it merged with the

San Antonio Gas and Electric Company to form the San Antonio Public Service Company.

December 2, 1959 〜〜〜〜〜〜〜〜〜〜〜〜〜〜〜〜〜〜〜〜〜〜〜〜〜〜〜〜

The city council scales back the plan for mass annexation. On September 10 the council had voted to annex 350 square miles, but then city leaders reconsidered, rescinding the ordinance and moving to annex half the area encompassing smaller sectors ringing San Antonio. The new city limits would landlock the municipalities of Leon Valley, Shavano Park, Hollywood Park, Hill Country Estates, Windcrest, and Kirby. "We pulled in our horns about 50 percent," City Manager Lynn Andrews said. "We did not feel, after further study, that we needed to get into the outlying areas." In a span of twenty minutes, on December 10, the council formally approved fifteen ordinances for the annexations.

December 3, 1869 〜〜〜〜〜〜〜〜〜〜〜〜〜〜〜〜〜〜〜〜〜〜〜〜〜〜〜〜〜〜〜〜〜〜〜

The Sisters of Charity of the Incarnate Word open the city's first private hospital, Santa Rosa Infirmary, with a ward of nine beds. On the first day eight were filled. San Antonio's population was twelve thousand at the time, and there was little means to treat the sick, injured, and orphaned. Earlier that year, a cholera epidemic swept through the growing city, prompting the order for the hospital. In 1930 the infirmary was renamed Santa Rosa Hospital.

Sam the San Antonio space monkey blasts off. The two-year-old rhesus monkey, raised at the University of

Sam prepares for space travel

Texas Balcones Research Center, was selected to study the effects of weightlessness on the body. After the launch from Wallops Island, Virginia, the monkey traveled fifty-five miles into the sky and spent twelve minutes in space. He then returned to San Antonio at the School of Aerospace Medicine at Brooks Air Force Base for study. Eleven years later he was transferred to the San Antonio Zoo and became a star exhibit.

December 5, 1835

The Republic of Texas army launches a surprise attack against the Mexican military in San Antonio. After two months of skirmishing with Mexican soldiers, the army was preparing to retreat to winter in Goliad. Ben Milam had other ideas. He wanted to attack before Mexican reinforcements could arrive in San Antonio. He offered his impassioned plea: "Who will go with old Ben Milam into San Antonio?" With three hundred volunteers, the army attacked at dawn. The siege ended four days later when the Mexican army surrendered.

December 6, 1918

Doctors urge the city to close public locations in the face of the Spanish flu epidemic. Four days later all schools and churches were ordered closed, and all dances and conventions prohibited. The numbers are in dispute, but local physicians reported more than twelve thousand cases of influenza, and of these, 881 people died—a fatality rate of 7 percent. Another survey found eighty-six thousand local flu cases and a 1 percent fatality rate. The Spanish flu is blamed for killing more than 2,100 people across the state and millions more around the world.

December 7, 1835

Ben Milam is killed by a sniper from the Mexican army during the capture of San Antonio. It was day three of the attack that Milam had inspired, organized, and led against the fortified Mexican forces there. Standing near the Veramendi house, Milam had been trying to observe the San Fernando church tower with a field telescope when he was shot in the head by a rifleman and killed instantly. He fell into the arms of Samuel Maverick. It is impossible to understate Milam's contribution to the cause of Texas independence.

December 8, 1939

Pandemonium erupts in a Bexar County courtroom when the not-guilty verdict is read for Mayor Maury Maverick, who had been charged with the crime of paying the poll tax of another. This was the fight of Maverick's life. Had he been found guilty, the penalty would have been two to four years in the state penitentiary. But what seemed to frighten the former congressman and full-time progressive was that he would be forced out of office and politics. This was made all the more serious by the fact that he was actually guilty. The International Ladies' Garment Workers' Union had shops in San Antonio. The New York office sent Maverick $1,000, of which he passed out $250 in silver dollars to the San Antonio workers with instructions to pay their poll taxes, which were $1 at the time. To top it off, Maverick did this in front of the press. Paying someone else's poll tax was a common practice for San Antonio's political machine. Maverick took the stand in his own defense and testified that he never instructed the workers to pay the poll tax and he couldn't have given the money to the workers since it was never actually his. He said he was only holding the union funds in trust and passing it back to the union members.

December 9, 1977

Students at the University of Texas at San Antonio select the roadrunner as the school mascot by a vote of 894 to 747. The option was more popular than the armadillo. Roadrunners, also known as chaparral birds or chaparral cocks, are a species of the fast-running ground cuckoos. The mascot was named during a ceremony where the UTSA band performed and a bonfire was lit. It was said that no other university had the roadrunner as its icon, but in fact a high school in New Mexico does. Fans would have to wait until 2011 to see the first UTSA Roadrunners football team run onto the field.

December 10, 1835 〜〜〜〜〜〜〜〜〜〜〜〜〜〜〜〜〜〜〜〜〜

The Siege of Béxar ends. For five days Mexican general Martín Perfecto de Cos was locked in street fighting against the Texan rebels. He had ordered his troops to retreat into a defensive position inside the abandoned Alamo mission. As the rebel artillery pounded the fortified mission, Cos prepared for a counterattack, but his cavalry officers refused their orders. Many deserted. With no options, Cos surrendered. He and his troops were allowed to return to Mexico on the promise that they would not fight against Texas independence again.

December 11, 1917 〜〜〜〜〜〜〜〜〜〜〜〜〜〜〜〜〜〜〜〜〜

Thirteen African American soldiers are hanged just outside San Antonio for alleged participation in the Houston race riot of 1917. The army held three courts-martial at Fort Sam Houston following the riot and found 110 African Americans guilty. They were part of the Twenty-Fourth Infantry Regiment Buffalo Soldiers. Nineteen soldiers were hanged and were buried in unmarked graves near the execution scaffold. Sixty-three received life sentences in federal prison. No white civilians were brought to trial. Shortly after the hasty executions, and in the face of condemnation from both military and civilian figures, the army made changes to its Uniform Code of Military Justice to prevent executions without a meaningful appeal. These changes remain in place to this day.

December 12, 1860 ～～～～～～～～～～～～～～～～～～～～

Lt. Col. Robert E. Lee hands the title of commander of the Department of Texas to Maj. Gen. David E. Twiggs. While Lee was in San Antonio he wrestled with his loyalties about the coming civil war. Torn about secession but in support of slavery, he engaged in thoughtful debate with staunch local Unionist Charles Anderson, who was in communication with Gen. Winfield Scott. Three months later Lee was ordered to return to Washington to assume command of the Union army. He decided he could not fight against Virginia and resigned his commission.

December 13, 1968 ～～～～～～～～～～～～～～～～～～～～

The U.S. Commission on Civil Rights continues its documentation of problems plaguing San Antonio's Mexican American community. Hearings were held at Our Lady of the Lake University for six days, from December 9 to December 14. Seventy witnesses gave testimony. Students explained their limited access to education; migrant farmworkers described harsh working conditions and extreme poverty. This was the first time any federal agency devoted resources to understanding the challenges facing Mexican Americans.

December 14, 1837 ～～～～～～～～～～～～～～～～～～～～

San Antonio gets its name. The Republic of Texas congress approves a charter incorporating the city, replacing the original charter granted to the Canary Islanders by the king of Spain. Ciudad de San Antonio de Béxar is renamed City of San Antonio. The city has had multiple names over its three-hundred-year history. The first formal census in 1788 refers to the township as the Villa de San Fernando.

December 15, 1966

A lawsuit is filed challenging the December 3 bond election to build the Tower of the Americas. San Antonians voted nearly two to one in favor of the $5.5 million general obligation bonds for the HemisFair centerpiece. The lawsuit, filed by nineteen petitioners who had opposed the tower project, claimed that the city council had violated the city charter in calling for the vote. Because the tower's construction had to begin in January 1967, the council invoked an emergency clause to meet the deadline, calling for the election two weeks prior to voting because two other attempts at financing the tower had failed. The lawsuit said this was not a valid emergency and the election should be voided.

December 16, 1929

A grand jury investigation begins examining the election of Augustus McCloskey to Congress. Allegations of tampering lingered over the November 6, 1928, election that saw Bexar County judge McCloskey, a Democrat, edge out incumbent Harry Wurzbach, the only Republican congressman from Texas. Claiming irregularities, Wurzbach contested the election and appealed his case to the Republican-controlled House of Representatives. After the investigation, the House reversed the election of McCloskey, who had served for eleven months, and seated Wurzbach on February 10, 1930.

Harry Wurzbach

December 17, 1949

The San Antonio Municipal Airport is dedicated. Mayor Jack White broke a bottle of Edwards Aquifer water to christen Terminal One and the administration building, which was funded with bonds voted on in 1945. In 1941 the city had bought twelve thousand acres of undeveloped land north of the city limit, but because of World War II it was used by the military as a flight training base and called Alamo Field. Terminal Two and the FAA control tower were completed in 1953. The airport saw its first major expansion in 1968 for HemisFair.

December 18, 1969

The film *Viva Max!* has its world premiere at the Central Park Fox and the Texas Theatre. Based on San Antonio native Jim Lehrer's novel, the comedy, about a modern-day general in the Mexican army who seizes control of the Alamo, starred Peter Ustinov. San Antonio filming of the farce became its own drama with vandalism against the film crew and the Daughters of the Republic of Texas protesting the subject matter. The Daughters declined to attend the premiere. The film was banned in Mexico.

December 19, 1832

San Antonio presents its list of grievances to the Mexican legislature of Coahuila and Texas. The document,

Representación dirijida por el ilustre ayuntamiento de la Cuidad de Béxar, commonly referred to as the Bexar Remonstrance, was drafted at the behest of Stephen F. Austin and signed by José Ángel Navarro, the alcalde of San Antonio. It sought statehood of Texas with separation from Coahuila and also sought to repeal a part of the law of April 6, 1830, that banned immigration from the United States.

December 20, 1836

Bexar County is created by the Republic of Texas. At this time Bexar covered almost the entire western portion of the republic, including the disputed areas of western New Mexico and northward to Wyoming. After statehood the vast territory began to be settled, and 128 counties were carved out of the area. The county was named for San Antonio de Béxar, one of twenty-three Mexican municipalities of Texas at the time of its independence. The name Béxar comes from a location in Spain that is a pre-Roman fort. In the eleventh century it was occupied by the Moors, and the name is rooted in the word "bees." It could mean "land of bees."

December 21, 1916

Emma Beatrice Tenayuca is born. The labor organizer, civil rights activist, and educator was the oldest daughter of Sam Tenayuca and Benita Hernandez Zepeda. Due to the family's poverty she was raised by her grandfather on the city's West Side. As a teenager she became a leader in a strike against the Fink Cigar Company. She is best remembered for her role uniting factions and organizing the largest pro-labor action in San Antonio history, the 1938 Pecan Shellers' Strike. Her efforts on behalf of the working poor earned her the nickname "La Pasionaria," or the passionate one.

December 22, 1883
A public posting is made detailing new city rules for public health and sanitation. The ordinance covered assorted categories of filth, cesspools, decaying matter, human waste, and other substances detrimental to human health. Household privies were required to be at least three feet from an adjoining lot, five feet from any street or public place, and ten feet from any ditch, river, or public stream. It was the home dweller's responsibility to maintain, clean, deodorize, and disinfect the privy every two weeks. Upon the receipt of a complaint the Board of Health could inspect any privy. Violations of the ordinance brought fines ranging from $5 to $200.

December 23, 1973
San Antonio's traffic director predicts that in the not-so-distant future people will park their cars and use a different means of transportation: the bicycle. The city

was developing an in-depth feasibility study of bikeways, or transit routes for those who like to pedal. A survey went out to the public seeking data to develop a plan. It was speculated the bikeways could make use of drainage and utilities easements and city streets. Feedback showed interest, but no funds were available to develop the bike paths.

December 24, 1854

Polish settlers arrive at what will become Panna Maria, the country's oldest permanent Polish settlement. Father Leopold Moczygemba led the 150 immigrants in the celebration of a midnight mass of Thanksgiving under a large oak tree. Three months earlier they had left Silesia and sailed to America, landing in Texas. From Indianola they traveled by oxcart to San Antonio and then to Panna Maria. In 1976 the community was included on the National Register of Historic Places.

December 25, 1868

During the middle of Christmas midnight mass, part of the roof and central dome cave in at Mission San José y San Miguel de Aguayo. This was one of many structural failures at the old Spanish mission. On March 9, 1928, the bell tower's south side collapsed. Some wondered if Mission San José was too far gone to be saved. The San

Antonio Conservation Society and the federal government pushed for its restoration, and it was rededicated in
1937. In 1941 it was declared a state historic site.

Mission San José, 2014

December 26, 1820

Moses Austin meets with Spanish authorities in San Antonio to ask permission to build a settlement in Texas. The Spanish government granted him permission to settle three hundred Anglo families after he promised that the settlers would be former subjects of Spain and would be willing to defend the land against foreign enemies. With the agreement in hand, Austin returned to the United States to recruit colonists but died on the journey back. The settlement scheme fell to his son Stephen F. Austin.

December 27, 1963

A Bexar County anti-Communist task force seizes books, letters, and other papers belonging to John William Stanford. The U.S. Subversive Activities Board ordered Stanford to register as a member of the Communist Party, and he refused. Using a general search warrant, authorities seized fourteen boxes of materials that included private documents and writing by Karl Marx but also some by Pope John XXIII and U.S. Supreme Court justice Hugo Black. Maury Maverick argued before the U.S. Supreme Court that the raid was unconstitutional, and the high court unanimously agreed. *Stanford v. Texas* was a major decision that laid out in clear terms that Fourth Amendment freedoms regarding search and seizure also applied to state governments. The Bexar County district attorney was forced to return all of Stanford's books and papers.

December 28, 1920

One of San Antonio's most prominent citizens, George Washington Brackenridge, dies at age eighty-eight. Brackenridge was a businessman, philanthropist, and regent for the University of Texas. His donations of time, land holdings, and wealth expanded higher education in the state and provided educational opportunities for women and minorities. He was also an advocate of women's suffrage. He organized two banking institutions in San Antonio and served as their president and was president of the San Antonio Water Works Company. His Fernridge mansion is part of the University of the Incarnate Word campus. Brackenridge Park and Mahncke Park were made possible through his donations of land holdings.

December 29, 1939

The San Antonio public library system reports that the year's most popular book was John Steinbeck's *The Grapes of Wrath*, which closely edged out Hitler's *Mein Kampf*. According to Grace Philippe, head of cataloging, Hitler's book had a prodigious run, but *Grapes of Wrath* had a waiting list of fifty and the library's eleven copies had "not been seen on the library shelves for some time."

San Antonians of the era preferred nonfiction books that covered history, economics, biography, and travel.

December 30, 2014

John Louis Santikos dies at age eighty-seven. The name Santikos had become synonymous in San Antonio with going to the movies. A Greek immigrant, he founded and owned Santikos Theaters, the largest family-owned theater circuit in the state. A year after his death the San Antonio Area Foundation revealed that Santikos had left an estimated $605 million to charity, the country's largest philanthropic gift at the time.

December 31, 1938

The day after a grand jury indictment is handed down for Mayor C. K. Quin, he calls for a quick trial to have the indictment quashed. After a lengthy investigation by the grand jury, Quin and two of his political lieutenants were indicted on five counts of misapplication of city funds to pay election workers. The indictment came. Porter Loring served as foreman, but Quin blamed Maury Maverick for the turn of events. The investigation found that some five hundred citizens were allegedly placed on the city payroll while employed as election workers for the "machine ticket," Quin's political organization. The indictments were thrown out on February 6, 1939, when Judge R. D. Wright of Laredo ruled that there was "no offense" and no law was broken. Quin lost the 1939 mayor's race to Maury Maverick. Two years later he was elected mayor over Maverick. In 1942 Quin resigned from the mayoral office to accept the appointment of judge of the Fifty-Seventh Judicial District. He died in San Antonio on June 18, 1960, while still serving as a judge.

Acknowledgments

Our profound gratitude to the journalists and story-tellers who shared their stories on the pages of the *San Antonio Express*, the *Light*, and the *Register*—all San Antonio periodicals that recorded present-day moments for posterity and contribute to our understanding of our city's history. Many thanks to the San Antonio Public Library's Texana and Genealogy Department. Finally, this project would not have been possible without the vision and support of Joyce Slocum, president and CEO of Texas Public Radio.

YVETTE D. BENAVIDES is a professor of creative writing at Our Lady of the Lake University and a commentator on Texas Public Radio. She contributes book reviews to the *San Antonio Express-News*, and she is the editor of Trinity University Press's series EQ: Creative Nonfiction on Social Equity.

DAVID MARTIN DAVIES is a veteran journalist with more than thirty years of experience covering Texas, the border, and Mexico. He is the host of *The Source* and *Texas Matters* on Texas Public Radio. His reporting has been recognized with numerous awards, including the 2019 national Edward R. Murrow Award for audio documentary.